Joshua

Courage for the Future

by Waylon Bailey

Adult Winter Bible Study
Convention Press
Nashville, Tennessee

How to Become a Christian

JERRY GAZA

Commitment is an important word in our society. We make a variety commitments in our lives—to a marriage partner, to an employer, to a mortgage company or bank, or to a civic club among others. The Book of Joshua reminds us about the most important commitment we can make, which is to God.

If you have never committed your life to God, you can do that right now. First, recognize that you are a sinner and need God's forgiveness. This involves repentance, which means to turn from or to change your mind about something. In this case you turn from sin to God because you have changed your mind about how to live. Instead of letting sin control your life, you want God to control it so you can live for Him.

Next, believe in Jesus Christ and what He did on the cross to provide salvation for you. This is sometimes referred to as placing your faith in Jesus. It involves making a commitment to Jesus, trusting Him to forgive you, and promising to live for Him.

Finally, confess your sin to God and ask Him to forgive you through Jesus Christ. If you ask, God will forgive you and you will be His child forever.

After this experience, you will want to tell others about it and get involved in a church. A pastor or another Christian leader will be glad to assist you.

PRODUCTION TEAM

MICHAEL FELDER
Biblical Studies Designer
WAYNE OZMENT
Editor
DAVID FOLDS
Graphic Designer
MELISSA FINN
Technical Specialist
ANGELYN GOLMON
Production Specialist

Send questions/comments to:
Wayne Ozment, Editor
127 Ninth Avenue North
Nashville, TN 37234-0175
or email: adultwbs@bssb.com

MANAGEMENT PERSONNEL

RICK EDWARDS
Manager, Adult Biblical Studies Section
LOUIS B. HANKS
Director, Biblical Studies Department
BILL L. TAYLOR
Director, Bible Teaching-Reaching Division

ISBN: 0-7673-3207-5
This book is a resource for Developing Teaching Skills course (LS-0053) of the Leadership and Skill Development category and the subject area Bible Studies (CG-0436) in the Christian Growth category of the Christian Growth Study Plan.
Subject Heading: Bible. Old Testament: Joshua
Dewey Decimal Classification Number: 222.2
Printed in the United States of America
Bible Teaching-Reaching Division
The Sunday School Board of the Southern Baptist Convention
127 Ninth Avenue North
Nashville, TN 37234

T A B L E

C O N T E N T S

We believe the Bible has God for its author, salvation for its end, and truth, without any mixture of error for its matter. The 1963 statement of *The Baptist Faith and Message* is our doctrinal guideline.

Unless otherwise stated, Bible quotations in this book are from the NEW AMERICAN STANDARD BIBLE, Copyright © The Lockman Foundation, 1960, 1962, 1963, 1968, 1971, 1973, 1975, 1977, 1995. Used by permission.

Do I Have a Future?

Scripture Verses	Joshua 1:1-18 (Focal: 1:1-18)

I cannot remember the exact time in my life, but I do remember this incident. Somewhere around my 12th birthday, I calculated how old I would be in the year 2000. I also calculated how old my parents would be. Even then I assumed I would be alive in 2000, and I hoped my parents would be. We all wanted to see one century and millennium end and a new century and millennium begin.

Early in life I wondered about the future. Now that I am older, I still wonder about the future. Events in our country and around the world in recent years have created more concern about the future. Sometimes I wonder if I have a future. The new millennium causes even more questions. If I do have a future, where can I find what I need for it?

A Glance at the Past (Josh. 1:1-2a)

People in all generations have wondered about the future. Can you imagine what Joshua and the people of Israel must have felt as they stood on the banks of the Jordan River after Moses' death? After 40 years of Moses' leadership, the people of Israel surely experienced some fears about their future. Who would lead them? Would God still direct their leader? Would they survive into the future?

Joshua had been the faithful servant of the Lord and of Moses. When others rebelled against the Lord, Joshua remained faithful (Ex. 32:15-20). He stood by Moses when the people rebelled and he stood courageously when the people buckled under the task of defeating the people who possessed the land of Canaan (Num. 14:1-10).

FOR YOUR CONSIDERATION (1:1-2a):

1. Why did God speak to Joshua?   *Faithful, obedient*

2. What questions do you think Joshua might have had when God spoke to him?

3. What is God speaking to you about doing?

*1. Faithful
2 obedient
3. follower
4. Available
Joshua would see vision through.*

In times of stress Joshua had passed the test of faithfulness. His greatest test lay in this pivotal time when Israel had lost its leader. How would Joshua react? Would he be able to lead the people into the future?

Thinking about the future is stressful for many people. They have many questions and few answers. They too need a word from the Lord. I can assure them they have just that in the Book of Joshua. What God spoke to Joshua then still has meaning to people today.

A Look Toward the Future (Josh. 1:2b-5)

He "misunderstood the past, miscalculated the present, and ignored the future."[1] This was written of one man from the 20th century. It could not be written of Joshua, however. He knew the past and appreciated the present and its opportunities. He also looked forward to the future.

Learning Activity 1

REMEMBER???

Moses, the leader for 40 years, was dead. Joshua was the new leader. He said in essence, "Get your supplies ready. We are going to cross the Jordan and take possession of the land." He then addressed the tribes of Gad, Reuben, and the half-tribe of Manasseh (Josh. 1:12-15). What are some possible responses to Joshua by them? To record your ideas, complete the following: "We made a commitment to Moses, and . . ."

1._____

_____

_____

2._____

_____

_____

3._____

_____

_____

4._____

_____

_____

Joshua knew Israel's future lay in obedience to God. God commanded Joshua and the people to cross the Jordan River and to possess the land. Notice the words of Joshua 1:3. God already had given the land to the people of Israel. God had provided for their needs.

God also gives us what we need to serve Him. He does this not because we deserve it but so He can accomplish His purposes through us. This was the case with Israel. As God had promised to Moses, He also promised to Joshua: "Every place on which the sole of your foot treads, I have given it to you" (1:3). The verb tense indicates that though the land remained to be taken by the Hebrews, it was as good as theirs, since this was in the divine purpose.

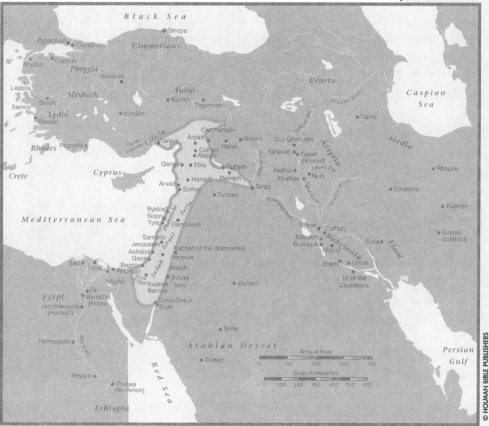

The light gray outlined area shows the great land promised Joshua.

7

God promised a great land to the people of Israel. While the description of the land is only outlined, it has enough detail to show the great blessings of God for a people who would obey Him. God would give them a land encompassing the area from the "wilderness" and "this Lebanon" (probably referring to the expanse of land running from the south and east to the north to the Euphrates River in the northeast and the "Great Sea" (the name then given to the Mediterranean) on the western coast.

The "land of the Hittites" probably indicated a people as well as an area. The Hittites had dwelt in the land of modern Turkey as early as the second millennium B.C. In later times the Hittites ruled over northern Syria. In the Book of Joshua the "land of the Hittites" probably refers to the area we know as Syria and Palestine.

For a people who had been slaves and without resources, the promise of such a land must have seemed only a dream. In reality this promise was completely fulfilled only in later times when David controlled all of the area.

God promised Joshua all anyone could ask. God promised that He never would fail or forsake Joshua and that no one would prevail against him. What else do we need for the future? The future may seem dark and lonely but God promises to stand with us and to never fail or forsake us. Even though we have no idea what we will face in the future, we have the firm assurance that God will face it with us.

For a number of years I taught at a theological seminary noted for sending missionaries throughout the world. As I looked into the faces of future missionaries, I assured them they could not go any place God had not already preceded them. The words of the Lord continue to each person who belongs to Him: "I will not fail you or forsake you" (v. 5).

FOR YOUR CONSIDERATION (1:2b-5):

1. What did God tell Joshua and the people of Israel to do?

Get ready to cross Jordan River into land God would give them

2. What territory would the people of Israel inhabit?

Every place they set foot from Lebanon to River Euphrates

3. Why is obedience important for believers?

As believers, we must trust God & serve Him — To obey God is to please God

8

4. Why do you think people have a hard time depending on God for all their needs?

Want to do things their way

As Joshua looked toward the future, he saw that God would be with him. God promised to go before him and to protect him.

Have you ever seen the Gateway Arch in St. Louis, Missouri? It extends more than 600 feet above the Mississippi River. You can ride to the top of the arch and look both east and west. On days the sky is clear, as guides there will note, you can see from 25 to 30 miles in the distance. Looking to the east you can see some of the territory early settlers crossed on their way west. Looking to the west you can see where they headed after they crossed the mighty river below you.

John 5:17

If you look back over your life, you likely can see how God has been at work in your life. If you will look toward the future and especially to areas of your life where you can obey God, you will have the same assurance as Joshua: God is already at work to carry out His purposes.

A Word for the Future (Josh. 1:6-9)

Three times God commanded Joshua to be strong and courageous (vv. 6,7,9). I do not usually think of courage as something that can be commanded. Nor do I think of strength as something we can make ourselves have. What did God have in mind?

God called for Joshua's obedience. If he used all his strength to obey the Lord, Joshua would courageously lead the people of Israel into Canaan. God previously had promised to deliver the people and to lead them into the land. More than anything else the people needed a leader who would obey and trust the God who would provide them the victory.

Consider our situation. We stand on the threshold of a new century and a new millennium. What do we really need? Do we need more technology or gadgets? Do we

Learning Activity 2

GOD WORKS THROUGH HIS PEOPLE!

God's plan was to lead the people of Israel to the land He promised them. Brainstorm ways God worked through His people to accomplish His plan.

1. Example: He provided leaders.

2. _Provided food_

3. _Provided weapons_

4. _Dried up river_

5. _Courage_

6. _Destination_

need more places to go or things to do? Or do we need to follow the plan of God that endures through the ages?

The word of God is as plain to us as it was to Joshua: "Be strong and courageous." We can be strong and courageous by doing exactly what God wanted of Joshua. We can use all our strength to obey the Lord and courageously do what He asks of us. This means following God's plan for our lives. In Christ God has given us the victory. We simply need to be strong and courageous in following His will for us.

Being strong and courageous involved obeying God commands (1:7). It still involves doing what God wants. It means having the courage to follow God. Many people model their lives after some contemporary person or group. Does it make sense to follow failed models? Wouldn't it make more sense to follow the perfect Model God has provided?

How much time do you give to meditating on the Scriptures?

God also promised Joshua that following His directions would lead to success. The promise was certain because God is the Lord of history. He promised to give the people the land. He gave instructions concerning how to take it. What would hinder this success? Only disobedience.

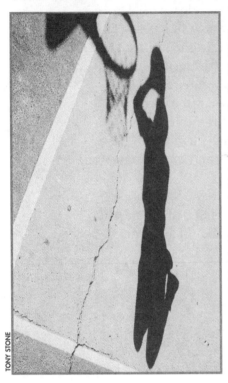

TONY STONE

What about your life? Since God has given you a pattern for successful living, what could hinder your success in life? Only disobedience can keep you from a life of meaning and significance.

God's words to Joshua mirror at least two ideas of Psalm 1. God wanted Joshua to meditate on the law day and night. In Psalm 1:2 "meditate" is used to describe an action of a godly person: "and in His law he meditates day and night." The word describes a low murmuring sound of a person contemplating something. The word also is used of the sound a lion makes over its prey.

Joshua 1:8 and Psalm 1:3 both indicate the godly person will prosper. Not long ago I read an article in *Sports Illustrated* about David Robinson of the San Antonio Spurs. After beginning his career in the National Basketball Association, David Robinson came to know the Lord. The article noted that Robinson now lives a life much different from that of many professional athletes. Then it pointed out that in life David Robinson prospers. The author put it this way: "Those around him might disagree with his beliefs and his words sometimes . . . but can there be disagreement with the way he lives his life? He walks through all the commercial hell fires that man has invented and comes out just fine. He prospers."[2]

FOR YOUR CONSIDERATION (1:6-9):

1. What was God's repeated emphasis to Joshua in these verses?

Be strong + courageous

2. What was to be Joshua's guide?

the law - God's word

3. What warning did God give to Joshua about obedience?

Be careful to obey that you may be successful & prosperous

4. What is the relationship between obedience and blessing?

Blessings come with obedience

5. Why could Joshua feel confident the people of Israel would be successful?

God would be with them

6. Why do you think God emphasized the need to be strong and courageous?

7. How confident of success are you when you obey the Lord's leading? Why?

8. If God told you to be strong and courageous in a particular matter, how do you think you would react?

God wants His Word to be a part of our lives continuously, "day and night." When we do so, He will make our way prosperous in all we do.

Preparation for the Future (Josh. 1:10-11)

After God spoke to Joshua concerning the future, Joshua began the process of preparing for the days ahead. While the victory had been assured, God did not promise ease. God would not reward laziness or failure to prepare. Joshua saw that a life of following God meant intense preparation and hard work. Following God's call means first preparing for the journey.

FOR YOUR CONSIDERATION (1:10-11):

1. How did Joshua show he had accepted the responsibility God gave him?

Gave orders to people

2. Why do some people tend to think they don't need intense preparation for God's service?

3. Should service to God be more or less demanding than service in other areas? Why?

more

4. Why is the call to serve God a call to prepare and train?

Preparation is essential to achieving victory, as any military leader knows. After describing what he had done in successfully preparing for the entrance tests to the U. S. military academy, General Douglas MacArthur wrote, "When the marks were counted, I led. My careful preparation had repaid me. It was a lesson I never forgot. Preparedness is the key to success and victory."[3]

Joshua knew the necessity of preparation in God's service. Do we? Do you? Obviously the first step in preparing to serve God is to become a Christian. What comes after that? Joshua shows us we need to prepare to obey God. Nothing is more important in helping us obey God than making preparation to do so!

Obedience for the Future (Josh. 1:12-18)

The land east of the Jordan had belonged to Og, the king of Bashan, and Sihon, the king of the Amorites; but all the people of Israel had helped defeat these two kings. The tribes of Reuben, Gad, and the half-tribe of Manasseh wanted the land of these kings because it was suited to raising cattle, which was their occupation. Moses had granted this land to these tribes based on their willingness to help the remainder of the people take the land west of the Jordan (Deut. 3:1-20).

Joshua 1:12-18 records conversations among the people of Israel concerning the commitment of the Reubenites, Gadites, and the half-tribe of Manasseh to help take the remainder of the land. These two and a half tribes already had a suitable place to live. They enjoyed a rest at possessing the land that the people west of the Jordan would not know for years. They covenanted with the other tribes, however, to follow through on their commitment. When the conquest was complete, these men then would return to their families across the river.

Joshua 1:16-18 can be understood in one of two ways. (1) It was the response of the two and a half tribes affirming their previous agreement to help take all the land of Canaan. (2) Or this was the affirmation of the officers Joshua sent among the people (vv. 10-11). They would obey the words of Joshua as they had obeyed Moses before him.

FOR YOUR CONSIDERATION (1:12-18):

1. Who received an inheritance of the land east of the Jordan?

2. What was expected of these people and their families?

15

3. How has God's emphasis on service and obedience affected your life?

4. How confident are you that you have a future? Why?

Either way, these people wanted to follow God. They knew the Lord would give the victory. While Joshua's leadership was important, God's leadership was vital. They would go anywhere Joshua led as long as he followed God.

God's leadership is just as vital for us. If we follow God, we can face anything with courage and confidence.

On visiting Russia a few years after the communist revolution, one man said, "I have been over into the future, and it works."[4] He thought what had happened in Russia was the future of the world. How wrong he was!

We have not gone and cannot go into the future. Yet we know it works, and for a far different reason than what this man thought. It works because of God who wants to lead us into it. As long as we follow His leadership, we can face whatever happens, even as we enter the next millennium.

---

[1]Harry S. Ashmore, *An Epitaph for Dixie* (New York: W. W. Norton & Company, 1958), 40.
[2]Leigh Montville, "Trials of David," *Sports Illustrated*, April 29, 1996, 106.
[3]Douglas MacArthur, *Reminiscences* (New York: McGraw-Hill Book Company, 1964), 18.
[4]Justin Kaplan, *Lincoln Steffens, A Biography* (New York: Simon and Schuster, 1974), 250.

CHAPTER

2

Does Obedience Matter?

Scripture Verses	Joshua 2:1—5:12 (Focal: 2:1—5:12)

A young mother in our church said that sometime after coming to know the Lord, she became convinced she should tithe. Like most people she wondered how she could afford to tithe but decided to obey God and trust Him for what she needed.

For a long time after her salvation experience she prayed for her husband. In the same month she obeyed the Lord and tithed, her husband expressed an interest in the Lord. Not long after that he trusted Christ. When she decided to obey God in her giving, she and her family experienced wonderful spiritual blessings. Because of her obedience, others in our church also decided to tithe. The final results of her obedience are not yet clear, but this much is obvious: God continues to bless those who obey Him.

Our church has learned a valuable lesson: obedience is the key that opens the door to God's blessings. Israel learned this lesson by following God's instructions about entering the promised land.

Step Forward (Josh. 2:1-24)

Jack Gulledge tells about a devout man who took as his life's motto a Latin phrase that means "He who does not move forward moves backward."[1] Joshua was certainly a man who moved forward. He also knew the first step in moving forward to serve and obey God involves preparation. Joshua had

JERRY GAZA

Obedience is the key that opens the door to God's blessings.

taken one such step in working alongside Moses. When he became the leader, Joshua led Israel to make adequate preparations to obey God.

Before the Israelites crossed the Jordan to take the land God had given them, Joshua sent spies to determine the important features of the land. Joshua planned to split the land of Canaan by entering the central region at Jericho. After securing this region, the people of Israel could move north and south without fearing that enemy reinforcements would hinder their advance. This plan meant capturing Jericho was the key to taking the land.

IN DEPTH

Jericho, one of the oldest cities in history, lay in the central portion of Canaan, just north of the Dead Sea and about 20 miles from Jerusalem. Excavations at Jericho still show some of the remnants of the huge walls that protected the city in ancient times. Fed by a large spring, Jericho was a prosperous oasis.

Entering Jericho, the spies took refuge in the home of Rahab. Because she had heard of the mighty power of God (vv. 9-10), Rahab believed in Him. The inhabitants of Jericho also knew about the exploits of the children of Israel. Rahab testified that Israel's success had come as a result of God's work (v. 11). God had led His people across the Red Sea and had given them victory over the two kings of the Amorites. Even the heathen can testify to God's greatness.

FOR YOUR CONSIDERATION (2:1-24)

1. Identify the main characters in Joshua 2.

Rahab (prostitute)
2 spies
Joshua

2. What did the two spies promise Rahab? What was her responsibility concerning the fulfillment of this promise? *To spare her life + her family*

Tie scarlet cord in her window
bring all her family to her home

3. What was the significance of taking Jericho as soon as the people of Israel entered the land?

To have a home and/or headquarters

4. How would you describe the faith of Rahab? Justify your answer. *Much faith*

v. 8 Believed they would succeed
Heard Lord had dried up sea

5. Why is preparation important to your service for God? *If not prepared*
— don't know best way + how to serve

6. How does preparing to serve God relate to depending on God for everything?

Preparing — Study God's word
+ pray — thus depend on God for help

The last part of verse 11 reflects Rahab's assessment of the Lord God. She described Israel's God as being "God in heaven above and on earth beneath." Rahab's faith in God seems far advanced over many of the Israelites in the wilderness. They had seen the work of the Lord firsthand and still failed to obey Him.

19

Rahab requested kindness for her and her family from the spies and their army when they attacked Jericho. She agreed to place a scarlet cord in the window of her house. When they attacked, Hebrew soldiers would see the cord and know not to destroy those inside the house. After receiving assurance of the spies' faithfulness to her and her family, Rahab then helped the spies escape over the wall of the city.

The two men returned to Joshua and reported on the situation at Jericho. They declared that God would keep His promise to give the land to His people and that the inhabitants of Jericho feared the people of Israel (v. 24). The Lord was with them just as He had promised Joshua.

Israel was ready to step forward into the future. Are we?

Follow Through (Josh. 3:1-17)

We do not know what the future holds. We need to remember God will lead us through it, even the difficult times. He will guide us so we can make it through life. Our part is to follow through on our preparation to follow God.

In a sermon on forgiveness I once challenged the people to admit it if they had done something "incredibly stupid" that had hurt another person and to ask for forgiveness. I also asked those who had been hurt to forgive.

In the sermon I told a story about a man in the Old West who was sentenced to be hanged for murder. Eventually the territorial governor agreed to pardon the man if he showed remorse. When given the opportunity, the prisoner showed no remorse and was hanged.

On the Sunday I preached this sermon, a family who had recently moved into our area was visiting our church. After the service the woman's husband said to her, "I've been incredibly stupid. Will you forgive me?" Her response caught him completely off guard. She said, "I'd rather hang."

Later she did forgive him and now their life is back where it should be. This family faced intense stress, primarily because of their move, but a family sickness had caused additional stress. The wife said she felt all alone and "like sawdust" on the inside. She added, "While I did not know the answer, I knew the answer was to be found with God and at church." She said if they were to make it as a family they knew they would have to follow God.

Joshua 3 is about following through on following God. To show the necessity of following Him, God gave the people of Israel a dramatic event at the Jordan River. Flowing north to south, this river is about 25 percent mud. It stretches over 200 miles from Mount Hermon to the Dead Sea, furiously plunging from several hundred feet above sea level to approximately 1,300 feet below sea level. At flood stage it is an imposing body of water.

FOR YOUR CONSIDERATION (3:1-17)

1. What was the purpose of what God did at the Jordan River?

Israelites would know God was with them + would drive other people out of land

2. What happened when the priests stepped into the Jordan River as they carried the ark of the covenant?

water stopped flowing

3. Why was following God a necessity for the people of Israel?

To receive their promised land

4. Why is following God a necessity for Christians?

To receive blessings

5. In what ways do you show you are following God?

Joshua commanded the people to follow the ark of the covenant into the Jordan River. The people lined up behind the priests who carried the ark. As the priests stepped into the river, the waters up- and downstream were cut off, and the people of Israel walked across the Jordan on dry ground.

IN DEPTH

The ark of the covenant, the original container for the Ten Commandments, was the main symbol of God's presence with Israel. As such, this wooden box was the most important object in the tabernacle during the desert period. It measured about four feet in length by two and a half feet in width and was two and a half feet deep. Two permanent poles were used as handles in carrying it (since no one could touch it). Several places in Israel—Gilgal, Shechem, Bethel, Shiloh, Keriath-Jearim, and Jerusalem—served at various times as home to the ark.

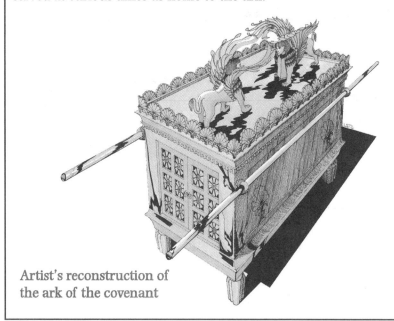

Artist's reconstruction of the ark of the covenant

Notice how many times the idea of "following" appears in this chapter. The people were to "go after" the ark (v. 3). They had to follow the ark because they had "not passed this way before" (v. 4). The priests took up the ark and "went ahead of the people" (v. 6). The people of Israel depended on God for their existence. Their lives depended on following through on following God. They knew it and did it.

Remember and Celebrate (Josh. 4:1-24)

Whenever one of our two daughters did something particularly well, we celebrated. When we had piano recitals or big tennis matches or a musical or drama, we'd go for ice cream. This celebration communicated that our daughters had done something significant, that it was an important event. By doing something special, we also expressed how much we cared about them.

FOR YOUR CONSIDERATION (4:1-24)

1. How were the people supposed to answer their children about the meaning of the twelve stones?

Memorial — When flow of Jordan was cut off - before the ark of the covenant of the Lord — What the Lord had done

2. By what means were the stones set up as a remembrance to the Lord?

By 12 men appointed from 12 Tribes

3. What is the significance of the two and a half tribes' crossing the Jordan River in battle array?

Moses had directed them

4. Why do you think celebrating successes is important?

5. Besides baptism and the Lord's Supper, how do Christians remember and celebrate what God has done for them?

Everyone needs to celebrate success. Individuals and groups alike need to celebrate their successes. This is true even of churches and nations. The Lord encourages celebration as His command to Joshua shows.

Joshua obeyed the command to help the people remember the significance of what the Lord had done in

Learning Activity 1

CELEBRATIONS AND MEMORIES

In column one list as many special events in life as you can. They do not have to be in chronological order. In column two give the way we remember them. An example is given in number 1.

<u>Special Events</u>:   **<u>Way(s) to Remember</u>:**

1. <u>Wedding</u>   1. <u>Wedding ring</u>

2. _____   2. _____

3. _____   3. _____

4. _____   4. _____

5. _____   5. _____

6. _____   6. _____

7. _____   7. _____

8. _____   8. _____

9. _____   9. _____

10. _____   10. _____

their lives. Joshua selected twelve men, one from each tribe. Each of them returned to the riverbed and chose a large stone. The men carried the stones to their next camp, where Joshua built a monument as a reminder of the miracle God wrought at the river. In later years when children and grandchildren would ask why the stones were there (vv. 6-7), the people were to tell them what the Lord had done. These stones would remind these and future generations that the same God who had led in the past would also be faithful in the future.

Children ask us wonderful questions. They ask sensible questions such as, Why do we go to church? or, Why don't we do the kinds of things other families do? or, Why do we *have* to go to church *every* Sunday? Answers to these questions communicate our faith and values.

What do you tell children about the
importance of attending church regularly?

Our children need to know our values. They need to know there are things about which we do not compromise. When we take the time to answer our children's questions, we express which of our values are truly important. We also communicate that they—the children—are important.

25

Learning Activity 2

AN ASSIGNMENT FROM GOD*
Joshua 4:1-7

Answer the following questions to learn what God's instructions were when the nation had completed crossing the Jordan.

1. How many men did God tell Joshua to choose? _12_

2. How were the men to be selected? _____
_____ Joshua choose them _____

3. What were the men to do? _____
Go in River before ark & pick up stone & bring back

4. How do we know the stones were large? _____
Take on their Shoulder

5. What was the purpose of the stones? _____
Memorial

* For answers, see inside of back cover.

We celebrate to remember the past and to look forward to the future. When I look to the victories of the past, I instinctively think of the possibilities for the future. For example, I think of the new millennium as another promised land God has given to His people. I believe if we obey God about taking this land, He'll give us the victories we need to accomplish this task.

The same God who led the people of Israel across the Jordan at flood stage can carry us through life. Storms inevitably come in life but we can have courage for the future because of God's faithfulness in the past. Even if our problems seem larger than those of Israel, all problems are small in the eyes of the faithful God.

Remembrance and celebration are important for two more reasons. When we celebrate our victories, we help other people know the hand of the Lord is mighty. Also celebration helps those who experience the mighty works to fear the Lord forever (v. 24). To fear God does not mean to cringe before Him. Rather, it means to hold Him in the highest esteem possible. It means to stand in awe before His greatness. When we remember and celebrate, we acknowledge the power of the One who gave the victory.

Give God Honor and Glory (Josh. 5:1-12)

God's actions on behalf of the people of Israel impressed their enemies. Joshua 5:1 mentions two enemies who knew they could not stand before the power of the One who dried up the river Jordan. This shows the inhabitants of Palestine had heard of the power of the living God who was going before His people to give them victory.

"Amorites" refers to those people who settled in the hill country of the land of Canaan. The hill country ran through the central region of the area on both sides of the Jordan River. Many archaeologists believe the Amorites were descendants of invaders from the northeast who came to Palestine as early as the third millennium B.C.

The earliest references to the "Canaanites" located them along the coast of the Mediterranean. Later the word became a general term for inhabitants of the land of Palestine. The Book of Joshua refers to the Amorites as inhabiting the central hill country and the Canaanites as inhabiting the Mediterranean plain.

IN DEPTH

Passover occurred on the fourteenth day of the first month of the year (our March or April). God called for the people to hold a seven-day feast beginning with Passover and continuing with the Feast of Unleavened Bread (Lev. 23:5-6).

Passover commemorated the time when the final plague came on the people of Egypt. God instructed the people of Israel to place the blood of an animal on the doors of their houses so the death angel would "pass over" the houses of the Hebrews.

The unleavened bread was the bread of affliction. It signified the haste with which the people of Israel left Egypt. God wanted the people to remember the time when He brought them out of Egypt (Deut. 16:3). By keeping the Feast of Passover and Unleavened Bread, the people would be reminded that "with a powerful hand the Lord" acted on their behalf. (Ex. 13:9).

The people of Israel had another opportunity to demonstrate their willingness to continue following God (vv. 2-9). They took full advantage of the opportunity. Joshua circumcised all the males who had been born in the wilderness. Israel's obedience to God's instructions concerning circumcision (see Gen. 17:9-14) showed their desire to let God lead them in the future. Obedience to God in the present demonstrates our desire to follow Him in the future. Thus the Book of Joshua once again shows us the necessity of obeying God.

FOR YOUR CONSIDERATION (5:1-12)

1. Why had the men of Israel not been circumcised?

Generation born while Wandering in wilderness

2. How did the people of Israel express thanks to God for His blessings?

Celebrated Passover

3. What was the significance of the Feast of Passover and Unleavened Bread?

*Remembrance of escape from Egypt
Blood on door post - death angel passover
Unleaved bread - Quick departure*

4. What are some ways your church could celebrate success and honor God in the process?

5. In what ways do you actively and explicitly express thanks to God for the ordinary things of life?

Praise

6. Why is obedience to God important?

God is pleased

Here at Gilgal, for the first time in the promised land, the people of Israel also celebrated the Passover. God no longer provided manna; the people ate the produce of the land for the first time (vv. 10-12). By being obedient to God and celebrating what God had done for them, the people honored and glorified God.

People need to remember and to celebrate. We need to give God the honor and glory due to Him. We all need to remember how the Lord has worked on our behalf and given us His blessings. The hymn writer wonderfully expressed this scriptural truth:

> Count your blessings, name them one by one;
> Count your blessings, see what God hath done;
> Count your blessings, name them one by one;
> Count your many blessings, see what God hath done.
> [Words by Johnson Oatman, Jr.]

---

[1]Jack Gulledge, *Ideas and Illustrations for Inspirational Talks* (Nashville: Broadman Press, 1986), 37-38.

3

Obedience Leads to Victory

Scripture Verses	Joshua 5:13—6:27 (Focal: 5:13—6:27)

B efore most of us can imagine, we will be trying to write and say the year 2000. Have you really considered what this new decade, century, and millennium will mean? Have you thought about what will be different and what will be the same?

What amazes me about the future is this: What we need for the future is what we have needed in the past. Our surroundings are vastly different from the days of Joshua, but our needs are the same. To write this material, I used a notebook computer. Later I communicated with my editor by fax or electronic mail. This material was printed on a laser printer in our office, copied with a high speed copier, and sent to the editor. All of these devices have been developed in my lifetime. Most of them came into use in the 1990s. When we think of these new inventions, we might wonder what in the world we could have in common with Joshua and the people of Israel.

What we have in common is human nature. The world's surroundings have changed but human nature has not changed. We have the same needs as Joshua and the people of Israel had. We stare into the year 2000 but we have the same human needs as those people more than 3,000 years ago.

Like Joshua and the people of Israel we need to know that we are not alone—that God will lead us along the way and give us His guidance. If we follow Him, He will show us His way. If we obey the Lord, He will give us the victory. Obedience leads to a life of substance and meaning.

The Assurance of Victory (Josh. 5:13-15)

Joshua was constantly reminded that the Lord gives the victory. The last paragraph of Joshua 5 records an unusual experience God gave to Joshua. Immediately before Joshua led the people into the most important military campaign in the land of Canaan, God appeared to Joshua in a special way. This experience reminded the new leader God was in charge and the victory would be His. The Lord wanted Joshua to see the necessity of obeying Him, of following God's leadership. If Joshua obeyed God and led the people to do likewise, they would have victory.

FOR YOUR CONSIDERATION (5:13-15)

1. Identify three important facts in Joshua's experience.

   Joshua was alone
   Joshua was reverent
   Joshua was obedient — removed sandals

2. What was Joshua's response in this experience?

   o Beyed   removed shoes
   worshiped

3. Why was Joshua told to remove his sandals?

   place standing is holy

4. What is the relationship between obedience and genuine worship?

   True worship is obedience
   from within — our heart

5. What does this experience of Joshua teach us about God's blessing for today?

   o Bey — will be blessed

I have learned one of the qualities every pastor needs is leadership. Though the church I now serve is made up of many people who lead major corporations, supervise many people, and make decisions affecting large amounts of money, our church

Learning Activity 1

GOD'S UNUSUAL PLAN*

Solve the simple crossword puzzle below to discover God's unusual plan!

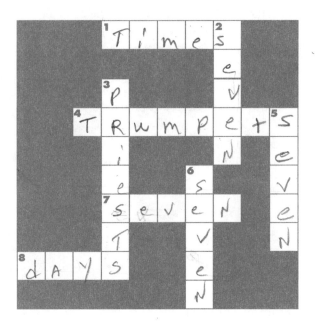

Across:
1. "On the seventh day . . . march around the city seven _____"
   (Josh. 6:4)
4. Instruments made of ram's horns (Josh. 6:4)
7. On the last day the people of Israel marched around the city _____
   times (Josh. 6:15).
8. twenty-four hour periods

Down:
2. The number for perfection in the Bible
3. Religious leaders
5. The number of days the people of Israel marched around Jericho
6. Jesus said to forgive 70 times ___.

God's Unusual Plan for conquering Jericho centered around the number ___7___. Leaders were to be _Priests_ rather than soldiers. The instruments of war were to be __Trumpets__ rather than swords.

* For answers, see inside of back cover.

needs leadership from its pastor. What should I lead them to do? More than anything else, I need to lead them to be obedient to God. As we are in tune with God and follow Him, the Lord will give the victory.

The experience also reminded Joshua that he would not lead the people in his own strength. Rather, he would lead the people in the strength God would give him. I am constantly reminded of how much I need the strength of God in my life.

As we read this passage, several questions may arise. Who was the captain of the host of the Lord? Why did Joshua respond as he did? Did Joshua worship the captain of the host by putting off his sandals? How are we to interpret this passage?

IN DEPTH

A theophany is a special appearance of God. Biblical scholars generally assume the experience of Joshua is similar to that of Abraham (Gen. 18:1-33), Moses at the burning bush (Ex. 3:1-12), and Gideon (Judg. 6:11-24). In each case the angel of the Lord appeared. The angel of the Lord has been variously interpreted as an appearance of the pre-incarnate Christ, the messenger of God who is so identified with the Lord that He speaks for God Himself, or as an appearance of God in some kind of human form.

Almost all interpreters agree this experience of Joshua was a theophany—a special appearance of God. I believe God appeared to Joshua in some kind of perceived human form. Please notice how I intentionally hedged in the language I used. Since we are talking about God, we should readily admit our human limitations. The finite cannot fully know the infinite. The human cannot completely know the divine. While the events and the meaning are clear, the exact interpretation of the captain of the hosts of the Lord is not.

The events of this experience are clear. Joshua was alone when he encountered "a man . . . with his sword drawn in his hand." Being a soldier, Joshua immediately issued a challenge. Was this one a friend or foe? The intruder identified himself neither as friend nor foe but as "captain of the host of the Lord."

Joshua responded quickly and properly. He bowed down and fell on his face. He also obeyed the command to remove his sandals. The presence of the Lord had made the ground holy.

The meaning of this experience for the people of Israel is also quite clear. The host of heaven would fight on behalf of Israel. Though the people were few in number and not equipped to overcome the well-fortified city of Jericho, the host of heaven would provide the victory. Though the enemy was great, the Lord God was greater.

After his encounter with the captain of the host, Joshua was ready for the battle of Jericho. His spiritual preparation was complete. Joshua's response at this point typified his behavior for all of his life. He sought to obey the Lord and follow His will. No wonder Joshua made such a good leader of God's people.

God is still at work in the lives of His people and He wants us to know that. He shows His power is available to us. He will guide us to victory if we follow Him.

The Way to Victory (Josh. 6:1-11)

Next, God explicitly assured Joshua of victory at Jericho (vv. 1-2). God then delivered the plan for taking Jericho. Capturing the city would depend on the people's obedience to the way set out by God.

FOR YOUR CONSIDERATION (6:1-11)

1. What did God command Joshua to do to capture Jericho?

    March around city 7 days – Then on 7th day march 7 times

2. Where was the ark of the covenant placed in the procession that marched around Jericho?

    Front - right behind armed guard

3. Why do you think God wanted the ark of the covenant in the procession going round the city? *Sign God was with them*

4. Why did the people of Israel carry out God's instructions even though they were unusual? *Believed God, Lord had told Joshua He had delivered Jericho to them. They had promised Joshua they would do whatever if He would lead them. Josh. 1:16-17*

34

5. How do you respond when God's instructions seem illogical or unusual? *Question if its God or not Run from it + tackle it*

Just as God gave Joshua an unusual experience, He also gave him an unusual plan. For each of six consecutive days the men of war were to go round the city of Jericho one time. In addition the priests were to "carry seven trumpets of rams' horns before the ark" of the covenant (v. 4). On the seventh day the warriors were to march around the city seven times, the priests were to blow their trumpets, and all the people were to shout (vv. 4-5). Then the walls of the city would crumble and the people would march into the city (v. 5).

Can you imagine how some of the people of Israel must have felt? They had trouble following God in the wilderness when there were no physical enemies; what would they do in the face of a powerful foe? God's plan must have seemed quite inadequate to these people. What did marching around the city have to do with taking Jericho? How would blowing a ram's horn make the walls of the city crumble? Following God's plan required both faith and obedience.

Some of us occasionally raise questions about what God tells us to do. For example, when God tells us to rejoice over the insults or persecution of others, we may wonder how we can do that. Sometimes the plan of God seems illogical. We often are tempted to trust in our logic instead of trusting in the Lord.

*1. Tim 5:19
Matt 23:11
Luke 9:23
1 Cor 6:*

When I pray, I sometimes want to tell God how to answer my prayer. I may pray something like this: "God, I've gotten myself in another tight spot. Will You get me out of this trouble?"

Not only do I try to use God to get me out of my trouble, but I also sometimes try to tell Him how He should act. I may go on and in essence pray, "Here's what I think You should do. In fact, God, if You'll just do it this way, everything will be perfect."

Regarding that kind of encounter I have to ask myself, Where is faith? Shouldn't prayer be a time of listening to God's plan rather than trying to plan for God? Shouldn't we pledge to follow God? Shouldn't we seek guidance from the One who led Moses through the wilderness and Jesus through the garden? Shouldn't we all follow God and do things His way?

The Timing of Victory (Josh. 6:12-21)

Israel's victory depended on God's leadership and the people's willingness to follow God's way. This victory also depended on their obeying in God's time.

When you pray, do you try to plan for God or do you try to listen for God's plan?

For six days the people of Israel encircled the city of Jericho. Each day they marched around the city once and the priests blew the trumpets as soldiers escorted them and the ark of the Lord. The people followed the instructions Joshua received from the Lord but nothing happened for six days. On the seventh day they all did as they had done before with two exceptions. This time they went around the city seven times and the people shouted when the priests blew the trumpets. Then the walls of Jericho crumbled. The people had continued to obey God and the Israelite men of war marched directly into the city.

FOR YOUR CONSIDERATION (6:12-21)

1. What happened to the items placed under the ban?

go into Lord's treasury

2. Why did God instruct the people of Israel to shout on the seventh day?

Shout " For the Lord has given you the city

3. Why do you think some items under the ban were saved from destruction and placed in the Lord's treasury?

4. Do you think God gives us the victory without our carrying out His plan? Why?

No

5. Why is obedience to God's way and God's time important?

What made the difference? Why didn't God give the people the city immediately? Why wait seven days when He could have given it to them on the first day? After all, God had said He wanted them to have Jericho. Did this plan help the people learn patience? Did it show them the importance of obedience? Did it teach perseverance and faith? Following God's plan in God's timing perhaps did all of these things.

IN DEPTH
The ban reflects two theological beliefs of Israel. (1) Israel saw the people and possessions of Jericho as a gift to God. Everything and everyone in the city belonged to God. The people of Israel dedicated these things to God, probably thinking of them as an offering to Him. (2) The people of Israel recognized that God had given them the victory over Jericho. Since the victory belonged to Him, everything captured in the victory also belonged to Him.

Learning Activity 2

BIBLICAL EXAMPLES OF OBEDIENCE*

Read these Bible passages and answer the following questions about each of them.

Scripture Reference:	Who was called to obedience?	To whom was obedience due?	What was the result?
1. Genesis 22:1-14	Abraham	God	God spared Isaac
2. 1 Samuel 16:1-13	Samuel	God	David anointed as King
3. Acts 26:12-23	Saul / Paul	God	Preached to Gentiles
4. Ephesians 6:1,3	Children	Parents	enjoy long life on earth
5. Ephesians 6:5-8	Slaves	Masters	Lord will reward
6. Titus 2:9-10	Slaves	Master	make teaching about God attractive
7. Hebrews 11:7	Noah	God	Saved family

*For answers, see inside of back cover.

The key element at this point was God's timing. This important truth will help us as we face the future. We don't know what life will be like after 2000 but we do know what God will be like after 2000. He will be the same then as He is now. God does not change. We can trust Him to work now according to His timing and we can trust Him to do the same in the future. What are you waiting on God to do for you? As you wait, look for opportunities to learn. God may be trying to teach you about patience, obedience, perseverance, or faith.

IN DEPTH

Holy War is a concept with which we are neither familiar nor comfortable. How could God's people utterly destroy other people and do so in the name of God? The wonderful revelation of God in Jesus Christ makes us wonder why God gave this command. Perhaps no explanation will completely ease our minds about these events but the following ideas are helpful: (1) The utter destruction of an enemy was a common practice among people of that era and that area. (2) Since idolatry was rampant in Canaan and produced some of the most abominable religious practices imaginable, this concept was a way of protecting God's people from paganism. (3) This occurred long before Jesus and His teachings about loving one's enemies. (4) This may have been God's judgment on Canaan. (5) As the Lord of history God was working out His purpose of choosing a people of His own and giving them a land of their own.

In giving instructions for the seventh day's march around Jericho, Joshua had relayed special instructions for the people of Israel. They were to take no spoils from the city. All of the inhabitants of the city and their possessions were to be placed under the ban; that is, they were to be consecrated to God. Nothing there was to become the property of the people of Israel.

Again the people followed God's directions. They not only marched around the city as instructed, but once the walls fell, they completely destroyed everything placed under the ban (v. 21). Their obedience to God resulted in the victory. How many blessings do we miss because we are not obedient to God?

The Results of Victory (Josh. 6:22-27)

The men who spied out the land had made an agreement with Rahab to spare her and her family from destruction. Rahab had been faithful to God; God would be faithful to Rahab as well.

After bringing Rahab and her family outside the walls of Jericho, the men of Israel set fire to the city. Only Rahab's family and the articles devoted for use in the house of the Lord were spared. Rahab's obedience and faithfulness resulted in God's blessings for her and her family.

What are you and your church doing that will make a difference 20 years from now?

God also blessed Joshua's faithfulness. Joshua had led the people through the years. God blessed him with success in his endeavors and with a name of renown through the centuries.

In younger years we often want the acclaim that comes only through a lifetime of service. We forget that Joshua's acclaim came only through years of devoted service to God. When we are faithful through the years, we will receive the respect of others.

I once saw this vividly illustrated with regard to a church's ministry. On a shopping trip my wife and I had the opportunity to talk for several minutes with a young clerk. She spoke of her family and her dreams for the future. She mentioned that many people left their children in a nearby day care center. This young lady stated she would leave her children only at the day care center of a certain church. Her reason: "because I trust them."

Interestingly she did not attend the church. Through the years the church had faithfully proclaimed the gospel and set the moral tone for the community. This faithfulness had resulted in a reputation that inspired the confidence of this young mother.

FOR YOUR CONSIDERATION (6:22-27)

1. List all that was not destroyed from the city of Jericho.

    Rahab + all her family
    silver, gold
    articles of bronze + iron

2. Why was Joshua effective as the leader of God's people?

    He was obedient & faithful

3. Where would you place Joshua in the line of great people of God? Why?

4. Why did Joshua's fame spread as a result of his leadership of Israel?

    Lord was with him

5. Why is obedience to God important for victory in our lives?

41

6. What are some victories God gives to people who obey Him? Which of these have you received?

I want my life and my church to inspire that kind of confidence. Here is a good question for each of us to ask: What is our church doing now that will make a difference 20 years from now? Another way to ask the question is this: What are we doing in our church that will outlive us?

Service to God always outlives us and brings meaningful rewards. When we are obedient to Him, we receive the blessings of a job well done. By being faithful through the years, we get to see many of the results of our labors. Jesus said the reward for good service is the opportunity to serve Him even more. "Well done, good and faithful slave. You were faithful with a few things, I will put you in charge of many things; enter into the joy of your master" (Matt. 25:21). Our reward will be the satisfaction of hearing His affirmation and the joy of future service for Him.

4

Disobedience Leads to Defeat

Scripture Verses	Joshua 7:1—8:35 (Focal: 7:1—8:35)

I once knew a person who experienced tremendous pain in her life. She had trouble in almost every relationship. She felt isolated and lonely. As a result she had to deal with depression and defeat in her life.

After I became her friend and learned more about her and the choices she had made, I became more empathetic toward her. I also became more realistic about her life. I eventually concluded that if I had made the choices in life that she had made, I would have been depressed too. She experienced so much distress and defeat in her life because she practiced disobedience.

We often will not admit that much of life is determined by choices we make. When we choose to live outside the will of God, we normally experience pain and defeat as a result.

Joshua 7—8 shows how disobedience leads to defeat. The people of Israel experienced defeat because someone disobeyed the commands of God. These chapters demonstrate in a powerful way that the choices we make help determine the kind of future we will face.

Disobedience Displeases God (Josh. 7:1)

Have you noticed that great problems sometimes follow great victories? Apparently success is hard to handle. For example, consider some companies that reach the pinnacle of success. They grow until they are larger and more profitable than any of their competitors. Then they forget how they achieved this success—for example, by customer service—and begin taking their customers for granted. Very quickly they are no longer so large or so profitable. They have great problems because they are no longer growing or increasing their share of the market. Sometimes people also have this experience. They cannot handle success and then great problems engulf them.

SELECTED CITIES OF CONQUEST IN JOSHUA			
City	Scripture	Occupants	Comments
Jericho	6:1-27	Canaanites	Rahab spared; Achan sinned
Ai	7:1—8:29	Amorites	Israel defeated at first for Achan's sin
Gibeon	9:1—10:27	Hivites	Became Israel's servants at worship place
Lachish	10:1-27,31-32	Amorites	Coalition partner
Eglon	10:1-27,34-35	Amorites	Coalition partner
Libnah	10:29-30	?	Levitical city
Debir	10:38-39	Amorites	Levitical city
Hazor	11:1-15	Canaanites	Largest city in Canaan
Megiddo	12:21	Canaanites	Guarded military pass
Tizrah	12:24	Canaanites	Ancient city

The people of Israel had that kind of experience as they moved from Jericho and attacked Ai. They went from the thrill of the victory to the humiliation of defeat. As Israel discovered at Ai, disobedience displeases the Lord. Achan had violated the command of the Lord by taking some things from Jericho that had been placed under the ban. His sin brought reproach on the people of Israel.

Notice that all the people did not sin. Someone has said everyone has the same beliefs about money, implying that all worship it. That often may be the case but it wasn't true in Israel, at least not on this occasion. In fact only Achan took the valuables (v. 1). His sin caused the anger of God to burn against the people of Israel and led to their defeat at Ai.

Through the years I have tried to help my daughters learn that the Christian life is the best possible way to live. I tell them: "Being a Christian and seeking to live for Christ will not insulate you from difficult times. But living for Christ will give you the best kind of life possible."

FOR YOUR CONSIDERATION (7:1)

1. What sin was charged against the people of Israel?

acted unfaithfully in regard to the devoted things

2. Why do you think verse 1 condemns all of Israel but mentions only one man's sin?

3. Have you ever experienced "the anger of the Lord" burning against you? What happened?

Think of all the ways being obedient leads to the blessings of God; then think of how being disobedient causes problems. Our society suffers devastating social problems because people disobey the commands of God. No wonder disobedience displeases Him. God has shown us the proper way to live. When we neglect His gracious guidance, we suffer for our disobedience.

Disobedience Leads to Discouragement
(Josh. 7:2-5)

After the victory at Jericho, the people of Israel felt invincible. After all, if they could overcome the fortress at Jericho, what could possibly stand in their way? If they had attributed the victory to God, their reasoning would have been correct. No one could stand before the mighty God who led the people of Israel.

When the spies returned from Ai, they exuded self-confidence. They counseled that not all the men of war should go against Ai. They thought they could take the city on their own.

Notice the contrasts between the campaign against Jericho and the one against Ai. (1) When the people marched against Jericho, they made intense spiritual

45

preparation. They obeyed God by circumcising the men born in the wilderness (5:2-9); and they observed the Feast of Passover (5:10-12). Before the campaign against Ai, nothing was said about spiritual preparation. (2) In taking Jericho the people followed God's plan. In the defeat at Ai they conducted the campaign in their own power rather than in the Lord's power.

FOR YOUR CONSIDERATION (7:2-5)

1. What happened at the first battle of Ai?

Israelites defeated by men of Ai Killed 36

2. What are signs the people of Israel had confidence in themselves rather than in God? *Not all people will have to needed only 2 or 3 thousand go up against Ai. No spiritual preparation*

3. Describe a time you or others trusted only in human power.

4. How have you or others demonstrated confidence in God?

Apparently the victory over Jericho gave the people a false sense of power. They assumed *they* had defeated the people of Jericho. They forgot the Lord their God. Moses had warned the people of just such an occurrence (Deut. 8:11-20). Unfortunately they succumbed to that temptation shortly after entering the land.

We too face similar temptations. We may think "my power and the strength of my hand made me this wealth" (Deut. 8:17). We easily forget the Lord has given us all the good things we have for a purpose (Deut. 8:18). We must remember the Lord our God who has blessed us.

This self-confidence and lack of spiritual preparation proved to be a recipe for disaster for Israel. Thirty-six men died at Ai (Josh. 7:4-5). The morale of the people, so high after the victory at Jericho, sank to the depths after the defeat at Ai. Note the beautiful but sad poetic description of their discouragement: their "hearts . . . melted and became as water."

Have you ever attended a church service after an ice storm had caused the electrical power to fail? When that happens, the thermostat won't work and the building is about as cold as the outdoors. No one would say, "Let's connect some flashlight batteries to the thermostat and we'll have heat in no time." That would be foolish because it still wouldn't provide the power needed. It is no less foolish to trust only in our own power and fail to make spiritual preparations to obey God. In fact it is not only foolish; it also is disobedient and leads to discouragement.

SW PRODUCTIONS

Have you discovered God's purpose for each of
the blessings He has given you?

47

Disobedience Leads to Despair (Josh. 7:6-9)

In addition disobedience leads to despair. The people of Israel had negative feelings as a result of this disobedience but so did Joshua. He appeared to have lost faith in God.

Despairing for himself, the people, and even for God, Joshua raised several questions in light of the defeat at Ai. For example he wanted to know what the defeat said about God. Did He have the power to lead His people? Had God forsaken them? Had God's name and reputation been tarnished? What did this rout of the Israelites at Ai say to the people of the surrounding areas? Would they take heart in this? What did the defeat say about the future of the people of Israel in the land of Canaan?

FOR YOUR CONSIDERATION (7:6-9)

1. How did Joshua and the elders of Israel respond to the defeat at Ai?

Tore clothes, fell facedown before ark of Lord sprinkled dust on heads - remained there till evening

2. How would you describe the attitude and emotions Joshua expressed to God after the defeat at Ai?

Defeated - complaining & questions

3. How do you respond to a defeat in life?

4. How can you improve your response to a defeat?

The Clear Fork Valley in eastern Tennessee once was known as the "Valley of Despair." People there felt trapped in their poverty and saw little hope of improving their situation. Finally after many years of programs and promises that produced no changes, a few of them decided to take action themselves. As a result , the situation there has changed and some now call this area the "Valley of Hope."[1]

Learning Activity 1

DISOBEDIENCE LEADS
TO DIRE CIRCUMSTANCES*

Read Joshua 7:10-21 and pages 50-52 of this textbook to find the answers to the following True or False questions:

____ 1. The Lord immediately identified Achan as the one who was guilty of sin.

____ 2. The Israelites were guilty not only of taking the devoted things but also of stealing and lying.

____ 3. The Israelites were then liable to destruction because the Lord was not with them.

____ 4. The first step toward reconciliation was for the people to consecrate themselves.

____ 5. When Achan heard God's plan, he realized he had sinned and immediately repented and was forgiven.

____ 6. Joshua was stern yet gentle when he confronted Achan.

____ 7. Even to the end Achan refused to admit his sin and refused to tell where he had hidden the devoted things.

*For answers, see inside of back cover.

Joshua knew how to move from despair to hope—he knew whose assistance to seek. He bowed before the ark of the Lord. Since the ark symbolized the presence of God, Joshua's action meant he was bowing before God Himself. Tearing the clothes and putting dust on the head were ancient symbols for mourning and repentance. Joshua and the elders of Israel mourned before the Lord and addressed Him with their needs.

Disobedience Leads to Dire Consequences
(Josh. 7:10-21)

God heard the cry of Joshua and the elders and began the process of restoring His people. God instructed Joshua to deal with the sin in a forthright way. His instructions show repentance requires actions as well as words.

Notice here the emphasis on the corporate nature of sin. God described how Israel had sinned. Though the sin came through Achan, in some sense all of Israel had sinned. They had transgressed the covenant with God by taking what was His as their own.

Have you ever had a virus that left you so weak you couldn't stand up? Sin is like a spiritual virus. It attacks us and produces dire consequences.

As a consequence of this sin Israel was unable to stand before its enemies. The people of Israel had the strength to stand against their enemies when they were willing to follow God; they were weak when they refused to follow God. The same is true for God's people today. Sin always weakens us. If we obey God, we will have the spiritual strength we need to serve Him. When we sin, we are weakened and subject to dire consequences.

FOR YOUR CONSIDERATION (7:10-21)

1. How did God respond to the questions Joshua posed in 7:7-9?

   Stand up - Israel had disobeyed & brought on the destruction

2. Describe the process God told Joshua to use in determining who had sinned. *Tribe by tribe*
   clan by clan
   family by family
   man by man

3. Why was identifying the sinner so important for Israel?

4. How do you deal with the temptation to acquire more things and to forget the things of God?

God instructed Joshua to begin the process of dealing with the sin in the camp. First the people had to consecrate themselves. Spiritual preparation is required for God's service but these people had failed to prepare. Second, God gave a plan to uncover the person who had sinned. This plan may seem unusual to us but it is consistent with how God revealed His will in biblical times (for example see Josh. 14:2 and Acts 1:26).

> IN DEPTH
>
> **The Urim and Thummim,** though not mentioned, seem to be in the background of Joshua 7. They apparently were sacred lots that would give a yes or no answer. The *New American Standard Bible* assumes the use of the Urim and Thummim by italicizing the words "by lot" (v. 14). The use of italics means these words do not translate any Hebrew terms.
>
> How these lots revealed the will of God is unclear. According to one suggestion, the Urim and Thummim were two flat stones with two identical colors on them, one on each side. If the two stones were thrown into the air and both fell with the lighter color up, God's answer was yes. If both fell with the darker color up, the answer was no. Presumably, if the colors of the sides didn't match, the stones were tossed again.

As God instructed, Joshua brought representatives of the twelve tribes before the Lord. He may have asked concerning each representative "Is this the man?" When the lots or whatever device Joshua used provided an affirmative answer, he then brought representatives from each family of the tribe and then representatives of each household and finally each household. By following the plan of God, Joshua eventually identified Achan.

I have always been amazed at how Joshua confronted Achan concerning his sin. He spoke with the seriousness of the situation in mind and with the gentleness of a kind pastor. As a result Achan confessed his sin, revealing in the process where the stolen items could be found. Achan described what often happens to people when they face temptation: "I saw . . . coveted . . . and took them" (v. 21).

Disobedience Leads to Judgment
(Josh. 7:22-26)

When the men of Israel went to the tent of Achan, they found the items exactly as he had said. While the value of what was taken from Jericho is irrelevant to the problem of obedience, the spoil represented a large amount of money. All the items listed in verse 21 had been taken from the Lord. After they were recovered, they were restored to Him (v. 23).

If you found a large sum of money, would you keep it for yourself or try to find the owner?

What happened next seems excessive to us and far removed from the way God has dealt with our sin in Jesus Christ. We may find other answers at a later time but for now the following ideas are helpful:

(1) The people of Israel viewed life from a corporate perspective. The whole family had participated in the sin and the whole family had to participate in the punishment. Considering where Achan hid the spoil, his family must have known what he had done. The sons and daughters probably were adult children since several generations could have lived together in the same tent. (Note Josh. 7:1 identifies four generations of Achan's family.)

(2) Sin is serious and cannot be glossed over. The people of Israel showed they took sin seriously when Achan and his family were stoned.

(3) The holiness of God must not be violated. In the wilderness the people could not touch the mountain because it was associated with God

and was therefore holy. Everyone in Achan's family and everything they owned was destroyed because all of them and their things had come in contact with what was holy, in this case with what was devoted to the Lord.

FOR YOUR CONSIDERATION (7:22-26)

1. At what place were Achan and his family stoned?

Valley of Achor

2. Why were the possessions of Achan and his family stoned and burned?

3. Identify different responses to sin given in Joshua 7. Compare and contrast them with your response to sin in your life.

Though we may still search for other answers, we cannot afford to overlook two truths that apply to us: Sin is still serious and the holiness of God is not to be violated. These truths warn us that disobedience leads to judgment. Israel experienced God's judgment in the first battle of Ai, and Achan experienced His judgment following Israel's defeat in this battle. If we do not receive God's forgiveness for our sins, we will experience His judgment.

Move Past Disobedience (Josh. 8:1-35)

I know a young man who has moved past disobedience. He went from despair and defeat to joy and happiness. Though he did not start out well, he seems to be finishing well. His bad start resulted from disobedience; his good finish is the result of repentance and obedience. He has courage for the future because he now knows the power of Christ to sustain him through life.

Chapter 8 shows Israel moved past disobedience in the same manner, through repentance and obedience to the Lord. In contrast to their earlier attempt to take the village, the people of Israel followed God's plan and captured Ai with relative ease. After hiding 30,000 of his men, Joshua attacked the city with a much smaller group. Again the men of Ai thought they were routing the Israelites and began to pursue them. With no defenders to oppose them, the rest of the Israelite army entered and captured Ai.

Learning Activity 2

CHOICES!

In the appropriate columns below, list choices you have made that significantly affected your life. Determine as best you can if they reflect obedience or disobedience to God. Describe the consequences.

Choices I have made	Obedient/Disobedient	Consequences
1.		
2.		
3.		

Israel celebrated the success by erecting an altar to the Lord and making sacrifices and giving offerings. Joshua also read from the law of Moses, perhaps from Deuteronomy 27—28, an appropriate passage for dealing with the need for obedience.

The account of Ai's capture reminds us that sin is serious and costs us. Obedience brings blessings, but disobedience brings defeat. A six-year-old boy had learned this lesson about his life. When it was time for his bath, his visiting grandfather asked, "Which shower do you use—the one upstairs or downstairs?" The child said, "Mother says for me not to use the shower upstairs, and when she says no, we'd better do no!"[2]

FOR YOUR CONSIDERATION (8:1-35)

1. Describe the plan Joshua used to take Ai on the second attempt.

2. How did Joshua and the people of Israel celebrate the victory at Ai?

3. Why do you think Joshua read all the law to the people when they had heard it many times before?

4. How has disobedience brought defeat in your life? How will you remedy this situation?

5. From your experience, how many examples can you name that show God blesses obedience?

This little boy knew what many today still need to learn. Obedience brings better results than disobedience. When God's people disobey, they suffer the consequences. When God's people obey, they receive His blessings.

---

[1]Jack Gulledge, *Ideas and Illustrations for Inspirational Talks* (Nashville: Broadman Press, 1986), 105.
[2]G. Curtis Jones, *1000 Illustrations for Preaching and Teaching* (Nashville, Broadman Press, 1986), 137.

CHAPTER

5

Look for Evidence of God's Power

Scripture Verses	Joshua 9:1— 11:23 (Focal: 9:1-27; 10:1-15; 11:1-6,15-16,23)

I received a phone call early one morning. A young man had died at home suddenly and since his wife had been attending our church, I was asked to come.

When I arrived at their house, some church members and neighbors were trying to comfort the grieving wife. We all did what we could to minister to our friend who had been shocked at the sudden loss of her husband. You can imagine how helpless we felt in such a difficult time.

Soon a team from the coroner's office came to do its job. I had dreaded hearing the investigator's mandatory questions, not able even to imagine how difficult they would be for our friend. I assumed the interview would be cold and sterile. To my surprise, the investigator spoke with compassion and genuine concern for her and the great loss she was experiencing. He was of more comfort to the widow than any of the rest of us there.

Later I talked privately with the investigator. I told him what a wonderful job he had done and how helpful he had been. Without hesitation he said, "It's Christ in my life." He then related when he met the Lord, even specifying the month and the year. He added, "You would not believe the change He has made in me."

The investigator went on to tell where he worshiped and the kind of service he performed through his local congregation. I left grieving for my friend but rejoicing that I had seen the evidence of God's power firsthand.

SW PRODUCTIONS

Where do you see evidence of God's power?

Joshua 9—11 shows evidence of God's power in fulfilling His promise to go before the people of Israel, to fight for them, and to give them the land of Canaan. By describing mighty acts of God, these chapters give evidence of His power. Here we read of the fulfillment of God's promise to Moses—to give His people the land of Canaan.

As I write these words, our church seems to be living from the Book of Joshua. We are in the process of relocating from our present facility—we have totally outgrown our space. We have bought land and begun the major tasks of planning new space and enlarged ministries. Our people constantly remind me of God's power. They say we need to plan well and be obedient and then get out of the way to see how God will do His great work.

As they faced the enemy, the people of Israel seemed small and insignificant; but God showed He has the power to keep His promises. The people of Israel needed to be obedient and then watch what God would do in keeping His promises to them.

Listen to What Others Say (Josh. 9:1-27)

When Joshua and the Israelites took Jericho, they had effectively cut the land of Canaan into two parts. Once they secured Jericho and then Ai, they concentrated on taking the southern and northern areas.

The Northern and Southern Campaigns *in Canaan*

God had told Joshua when they took the land, they were to utterly destroy the Amorites. This backdrop helps us understand the events described in Joshua 9. Verses 1-2 indicate the kings "beyond the Jordan" (that is, those living in the area we normally would designate as the land of Israel) united to fight against the people of Israel. These kings were from all three areas of the country and opposed Israelite expansion into the land of Canaan.

In the meantime the people of Gibeon devised another plan. They approached the people of Israel pretending to be what the Israelites really were, strangers in the land of Canaan. Their deception was well conceived and brilliantly carried out. Everything about the people of Gibeon looked the part of sojourners who had made a long trip to Canaan.

The people of Israel must have seen themselves in these travelers. After all, they recently had completed the same kind of journey. Like these travelers, the Israelites ate stale bread and wore clothes that once had been new but now were almost worn out. No wonder they believed the tales of the people of Gibeon!

FOR YOUR CONSIDERATION (9:1-27)

1. Describe the plan the people of Gibeon used in deceiving the Israelites.

   Dressed in worn-out clothes + shoes, stale bread + cracked wineskins to pretend they were from a long distance

2. Why did the Israelites feel obligated to spare the people of Gibeon?

   They associated them with themselves traveling a long way

3. What happened to the people of Gibeon after their plan was discovered?

   cursed - made woodcutters + water carriers

4. Why do you think the Israelites didn't seek a word from God before making a covenant with the people of Gibeon?

5. Do you think the people of Gibeon impressed the Israelites more by their old apparel and supplies or their references to God's acts? Why?

6. On what occasions have others called your attention to evidence of God's power? Have any of these people been unbelievers?

7. What were the results when you or your church failed to seek God's guidance about an important decision?

The men of Gibeon (called Hivites in v. 7) met Joshua at Gilgal and asked to make a covenant with Israel. Covenants, which established relationships between people or groups of people, were common in the world of the Old Testament. Therefore, both the people of Gibeon and the Israelites knew of covenants and their importance.

SELECTED COVENANTS IN THE BIBLE		
Scripture	**Parties**	**Comments**
Genesis 9:9-17	God, Noah	Covenant not to repeat flood
Genesis 15:18; 17:2	God, Abraham	Covenant of divine promises
Genesis 21:22-34	Abraham, Abimelech	Covenant of equals
Exodus 19:4-6	God, Israel	Covenant of chosen people
Joshua 9	Israel, Gibeon	Covenant based on deceit
1 Samuel 18:3; 23:18	David, Jonathan	Covenant of friendship
2 Samuel 23:5	God, David	Covenant of David's rule
Jeremiah 31:31-34	God, believers	New covenant promised
1 Corinthians 11:25	God, believers	New covenant fulfilled

The saddest words of this whole account are probably those found in verse 14. Joshua and the people of Israel "did not ask for the counsel of the Lord." How often we make terrible mistakes in life simply because we do what seems right in our own eyes rather than asking God what's right.

When Joshua confronted the people of Gibeon with their deception, they confessed their guilt. He then consigned them to performing menial tasks (v. 27). They would serve the people of Israel in the house of the Lord.

IN DEPTH

Covenants are agreements between two parties who may or may not be equals. The most familiar covenants in the Old Testament include those between God and certain people or the nation Israel. Jeremiah referred to a new covenant, a prophecy that was fulfilled through Jesus Christ. In biblical times covenants between people as well as between God and a person or nation were usually sealed by sacrificing an animal. Often the animal was cut in half and those making the covenant passed between the two halves. This practice conveyed the idea that anyone who violated the covenant would end up like the animal—cut in half! This helps explain why the people of Israel felt the need to keep the covenant with the people of Gibeon even when it had been made in deception.

Joshua had asked these people why they deceived the people of Israel. Their answer revealed the power of God and the ability even of pagans to recognize God's majesty and power. They had heard of the mighty works of God in the wilderness and how God had promised Moses to give the people of Israel a land. These pagans believed God!

Evidence of God's power is all around us. As we recognize it, we find strength for each day and encouragement for the future. One place to find that evidence may be in the words of others. Have you ever heard unbelievers describe God's work in their lives? Have you ever listened to them to find evidence of God's power? Of course Christians also frequently tell us about God's power.

As a device to keep his audience's attention, a preacher would stop at various intervals in his sermon and say,

"Listen. Are you listening?"[1] I assume he found this device to be quite effective for he typically used it as he preached. What he said to his congregation applies to us: "Listen. Are you listening?" When we listen to what other people say, both believers and unbelievers, we often will hear about evidence of God's power.

Stop for a Word from God (Josh. 10:1-15)

Joshua 10 shows how God promised and exhibited His power. He fulfilled His promise to deliver His people. Throughout the chapter we read that God gave victory to the people of Israel against superior numbers and fortified cities.

When the king of Jerusalem assessed his situation, he knew drastic measures were needed. Israel had taken the fortress of Jericho and the village of Ai. Even Gibeon had capitulated to the Israelites. Thus Adoni-zedek knew he would have to come up with a strategy to defeat the people of Israel.

FOR YOUR CONSIDERATION (10:1-15)

1. Describe how God showed His power in the battle against the five kings. *Attacked by surprise Lord threw them into confusion*

2. Why were the people of Israel able to defeat the five-king coalition?

   Sun & Moon stood still
   Large hailstones

3. In what area of Canaan did these five kings live?

4. What does the way God worked to defeat the enemies of Israel indicate about how He watches over His people?

5. Why do you think "the book of Jashar" is mentioned in the Bible?

6. How has God revealed Himself in your life? How has this provided evidence of His power?

7. What implications for your life can you draw from the account of the sun and moon standing still?

Adoni-zedek therefore devised a plan to unite the large cities of southern Canaan against Israel. The kings of Hebron, Jarmuth, Lachish, and Eglon agreed to fight with the king of Jerusalem against Israel and to begin by besieging Gibeon. Because of their treaty-covenant, the people of Israel were bound to defend Gibeon. Thus Joshua assembled his men and began marching them to Gibeon.

God reassured Joshua the victory would be Israel's: "Do not fear them, for I have given them into your hands; not one of them shall stand before you" (v. 8).

Two researchers discovered the reason the home team in any athletic event wins more often than the visiting team. It has nothing to do with their being at home or being more familiar with the facilities. The home team has more fans and therefore more vocal support. As their fans cheer and applaud them, the home team is encouraged and motivated.[2] How much more true this is of a word from God. When we stop to listen, He will speak to us—perhaps not audibly but clearly nevertheless. Best of all, whatever God says will encourage us. At the least He will tell us we have no reason to fear, that He is at work on our behalf.

Notice what happened each time God told Joshua not to fear for He had given the victory. (1) God did indeed give the victory. When God promised the victory, the victory came. God is faithful to His promises and faithful to His people. All Israel had to do to see the evidence of God's

Learning Activity 1

EVIDENCE OF GOD'S POWER THEN*

Match the following questions and answers to discover evidence of God's power as described in Joshua 10.

Questions:

____ 1. What news alarmed Adoni-zedek, the king of Jerusalem?

____ 2. To whom did Adoni-zedek appeal for help?

____ 3. What battle plan did the kings devised against Joshua?

____ 4. What message of encouragement did the Lord give Joshua?

____ 5. How did Joshua get the advantage in the battle?

____ 6. What killed more of the enemy than the soldiers of Israel?

____ 7. What was unusual about this particular day?

____ 8. Where did Joshua and the Israelites camp?

____ 9. What are Libnah, Lachish, Eglon, Hebron, and Debir?

____ 10. What was the key to Joshua's leading Israel to conquer all this land in just one campaign?

Answers:

  a. The element of surprise

  b. Gilgal

  c. The capture of Ai and the treaty with the people of Gibeon

  d. The Lord God of Israel would fight for Israel.

  e. Besieged Gibeon to draw Joshua into battle

  f. Southern cities Joshua destroyed

  g. Do not be afraid. I have given them to you.

  h. Hailstones from the Lord

  i. Five kings of the Amorites

  j. The sun and the moon stopped in the middle of the sky.

* For answers, see inside of back cover.

power was to watch the events of the day. God led the people and gave them the victory. (2) Each time God spoke with Joshua, Joshua then instituted a masterful plan and victory followed. While the Book of Joshua does not generally say that the Lord gave the plan, it always gives the message of God (for example, see v. 8). Does this mean God inspired Joshua with the plan he used? Or could it be God gave Joshua an explicit plan? While we do not know the answer to these questions, we can easily see Joshua and the people of Israel stopped long enough to get a word from God.

Afterward Joshua and his army journeyed all night and surprised the five kings besieging Gibeon. God showed His power and favor by confounding the enemy forces before Israel (v. 10). As the enemy fled, "the Lord threw large stones from heaven on them" (v. 11). This phrase is explained as large hailstones. More of the enemy army died from the hailstones than from fighting the Israelites.

During the battle Joshua prayed for the power of the Lord to come on the people and to give them extraordinary time to defeat the enemies of the Lord. Joshua prayed for the sun and the moon to stand still in the sky and to give the men of Israel a day like no other. Later the day is described as one that had not been seen before or since, a day when the Lord fought for Israel (v. 14).

IN DEPTH

The book of Jashar is mentioned at least two times in the Old Testament (Josh. 10:13; 2 Sam. 1:18). In both instances the book quotes poetic accounts of battles. On this basis many biblical scholars think the book of Jashar contained poetic accounts of events that were important to the history of Israel. These accounts were probably compiled during or just after the time of David.

With Gibeon secure, the people of Israel began systematically to take the southern part of the land. The five kings escaped to a cave where they were trapped (vv. 16-21). This left the king's armies without leadership and

Israel was able to cut them off before they could retreat to the fortified cities. After this victory all the kings were killed (vv. 22-27). Next Joshua and the people of Israel began to move through the southern area of the land, taking control of most of the countryside and many of the villages, towns, and cities. Joshua 10:28-43 summarizes the victory the Lord gave the Israelites. Though they did not attack every city, they did accomplish the purpose of taking the land.

Look How God Makes a Way (Josh. 11:1-6,15-16,23)

Reading the Book of Joshua gives us a renewed appreciation of how God works through people such as Joshua to accomplish His purpose. Israel's taking the land of Canaan involved brilliant strategy and precise execution. Over all of this, God was at work leading the way. In every place the people went, they saw evidence of God's power.

FOR YOUR CONSIDERATION (11:1-6,15-16,23)

1. Joshua 11 focuses on the Israelites' capturing what area of the land of Canaan?

2. What were God's instructions about taking this area of Canaan?

3. Describe the results of this battle.

4. Based on Joshua 1—11, how would you rate Joshua as a tactician and leader?

5. In what ways do you see God leading in your church?

6. How is God leading in your life?

7. What evidence of God's power do you see in your life and church?

Much like the kings of the south, those in the northern part of the country joined together in hopes of defeating the people of Israel. The names of most of the places identified in this chapter are less familiar to us than those of the southern part of the country, but they are generally located in the northern section of Canaan.

Despite any obstacle, God makes a way for His people.

As with the coalition of the five kings of the south, Joshua used a surprise attack against the coalition of northern kings. Joshua was a take-charge person who did not wait for events to control him. Instead he sought to control the events under the sovereignty of God. He had good reason for doing so for once again God had promised to protect Joshua and to give him victory over his enemies. God also had commanded Joshua not to be afraid.

Learning Activity 2

EVIDENCE OF GOD'S POWER TODAY

1. What evidence of God's power do you see in others' lives (or what evidence have others told you about)?

2. What evidence of God's power do you see in your life?

3. What evidence of God's power do you see in churches today?

4. Where else do you see evidence of God's power?

We can easily recognize the evidence of God's power throughout these chapters about the capture of Canaan. The Israelites took this land because God gave them the victory. "So Joshua took the whole land, according to all that the Lord had spoken to Moses, and Joshua gave it for an inheritance to Israel according to their divisions by their tribes" (v. 23).

In our worship services we often sing that "God will make a way when there seems to be no way."[3] This song reminds us that God leads His people. When the obstacles seem too great, God leads His people and makes a way for them. As you and I face the future, we can take hope in knowing God led His people in the past. We can confidently expect God to give us courage and guidance for the future as well.

---

[1]Herschel H. Hobbs, *My Favorite Illustrations*, Ronald K. Brown, comp. (Nashville: Broadman Press, 1990), 209.
[2]Jack Gulledge, *Ideas and Illustrations for Inspirational Talks* (Nashville: Broadman Press, 1986), 43.
[3]Don Moen, "God Will Make a Way."
© 1990 Integrity's Hosanna! Music/ASCAP
All Rights Reserved. Used By Permission.

CHAPTER

6

Remember God Keeps His Promises

Scripture Verses — Joshua 12:1—14:15 (Focal: 12:1,7-8; 13:1-8; 14:1-15)

My wife and I grew up in a small town less than a two-hour drive from some of the most beautiful beaches on the Gulf of Mexico. We could drive to the beach and spend a wonderful day in the sun, sand, and water.

Even though we have not lived in that town for a long time, we still think summer is incomplete without a trip to that same beach. We instilled a love for the water and sand in our two children. Almost every summer includes at least one trip to the beach.

We started our family out early with this tradition. I still remember one time we planned a several-day trip to the beach. We let the excitement build with our daughter. We counted down the days until we would leave for swimming and fun. Then literally as we packed the car, the phone rang. A member of the church had died. The memorial service would be held the next day.

Although missing a few days of vacation does not qualify for one of the great tragedies of life, I still dreaded telling our five-year-old child that the trip to the beach had been canceled. That doesn't seem like a big thing now but it was major back in those days.

Why was it so important? I wanted my daughter to know that her father kept his promises. I wanted her to know that she could count on me.

God's promises are as sure as the waves on the ocean.

You and I need to remember that God is faithful and we can count on our Heavenly Father. As we face the new millennium, we can find courage for the future because our Heavenly Father keeps His promises.

Promises from the Past (Josh.12:1,7-8)

God has always fulfilled His promises. God had promised Abraham that his descendants would be numerous, would sojourn in Egypt for 400 years, and then would return to the land of Canaan (Gen. 15:5,13-16). Moses was promised the people of Israel would be delivered from the oppression of the pharaoh of Egypt and be given the land of Canaan (Ex. 3:7-8). To Joshua God said He had given the land into the Israelites' hands (Josh. 1:5-6). Joshua 12—14 shows God kept all these promises. These chapters summarize what happened in Canaan after Israel entered it. Here we read about the land that was taken, the land that was yet to be taken, and the beginning of the apportionment of the land among the tribes of Israel.

FOR YOUR CONSIDERATION (12:1,7-8)

1. What were the boundaries of the area east of the Jordan?

2. What were the boundaries of the area west of the Jordan?

3. For what purpose do you think chapter 12 lists all the kings in the promised land whom the people of Israel defeated through God's power?

4. Who are some of the "kings" over whom God has given you the victory?

5. What are some promises God has made to your church?

6. How have you benefited from the promises God made to your church?

Joshua 12 tells about the victories of the people of Israel in Canaan under the leadership of Moses (vv. 1-6) and Joshua (vv. 7-24). Moses had led the people of Israel out of Egypt and into the wilderness of Sinai. Then he led the people to the east side of the Jordan where God gave them the victory over those who lived there. Verse 1 describes the natural boundaries of this area. The land extended from Mount Hermon in the north to the Arnon Valley in the south. The Jordan Valley, here called "the Arabah," formed the western boundary. The east side really had no natural boundary. It simply trailed off into desert.

Verses 2-6 name the kings east of the Jordan defeated under the leadership of Moses. God had promised their land to the Reubenites, the Gadites, and the half-tribe of Manasseh. The remainder of the chapter lists kings to the west of the Jordan. The 31 kings named here fell to Israel under the leadership of Joshua. Note the chronological arrangement of this list. Jericho and Ai were part of the central campaign and were defeated first. The next portion of the list gives kings who were defeated in the southern campaign (vv. 9-16a) and the list concludes with the kings defeated in the rest of the central campaign and in the northern campaign (vv. 16b-24).

God had promised He would give all of the inhabitants in the land of Canaan into the hands of Israel. God had promised the land east of the Jordan to the two and a half tribes. Joshua 12 shows that God kept all His promises from the past.

By looking to our past, we also can see the promises of God and that He fulfilled them. The same God who led us in the past will lead us in the future. As we consider God's provision at other times, we can take hope for His provision in the days ahead. Do you remember the song, "O God, our help in ages past, Our hope for years to come" (words by Isaac Watts)? That song expresses the relationship between God's help in the past and His promise of help in the future. That God kept His promises in the past assures us He also will keep His promises in the future. We can count on God!

Promises That Keep Coming (Josh. 13:1-8)

The same God who helped the people of Israel take the initial part of Canaan would help them take the remainder of the land. Joshua 13:1-8 basically concerns the part of the land not yet taken. Verses 1-7 describe this remaining part while verse 8 begins the description of the land given to the tribes of Gad and Reuben and to the half-tribe of Manasseh.

The events of the Book of Joshua occurred between the time of the wilderness journey recorded in Exodus—Deuteronomy and the time of the judges and the rise of Samuel. We do not know the length of the time period between the taking of Jericho at the beginning of the conquest and the statement that Joshua was old and advanced in years (Josh. 13:1). Caleb's later statement (14:10) may mean that it was only a few years.

Joshua 13:2-6 can be divided into two parts: (1) a description of the land remaining to be taken in the south (vv. 2-3), and (2) a description of the land remaining to be taken in the north (vv. 4-6). In the south the Philistine lords controlled five cities (v. 3) on the southwest coast. The Philistines, Israel's most persistent enemies, were not subdued until the time of David. "Shihor"originally meant the Nile River, but the

KEY IDEAS ABOUT GOD IN JOSHUA	
Idea	**Scripture**
God works through people	Joshua 1:5
God acts on behalf of His people	Joshua 1:5
God is sovereign	Joshua 2:11
God keeps His promises	Joshua 21:45
God punishes sin	Joshua 23:16
God alone is to be worshiped	Joshua 24:14
God is holy	Joshua 24:19

geography mentioned in this passage could indicate the writer had in mind a body of water on the Egyptian border, possibly the brook of Egypt (see 15:47). In the north, lands near modern Lebanon remained unconquered. This included the area around Mount Hermon, Sidon, and Lebo-hamath (the entrance of Hamath), all of which lay far to the north.

FOR YOUR CONSIDERATION (13:1-8)

1. What areas of the land of Canaan had not been taken by the people of Israel?

2. How do you explain that all of Canaan was not conquered under Joshua's leadership?

3. Why do you think the Book of Joshua describes the land that was taken and then describes what was not taken?

4. In your estimation why did God tell Joshua to apportion the land before all of it was conquered?

5. What does knowing God's promises were fulfilled in the past tell us about God's promises for the future?

6. How would you describe God's faithfulness to keep His promises?

7. What new promises are you anticipating God will fulfill in the future?

The land that had been taken represented no small feat and this description of what remained showed there was still much to be done. Best of all, God gave the people another promise. He would give them this land too.

There is always more that God wants to do for His people. He is working now to fulfill His promises to us. For example, Jesus promised He would always be with us (Matt. 28:20) and that the Holy Spirit would guide us "into all the truth" (John 16:13). Herschel Hobbs said he and his wife visited Jaipur, India, late one evening but they weren't allowed in one of the temples there. They were told the god was asleep.[1] In contrast, our God never sleeps. He is always in the process of fulfilling these and other promises to us.

Though all of the land had not been taken, the Lord commanded Joshua to allot the land to each of the tribes, which he did (13:7-33). As they had been promised, the tribes of Gad, Reuben, and the half-tribe of Manasseh received their inheritance east of the Jordan. Moses had promised them this inheritance and Joshua confirmed they would receive it once the land west of the Jordan was conquered (1:12-15).

Promises for Individuals (Josh. 14:1-15)
Joshua 14, a stirring passage of Scripture, tells the wonderful story of Caleb. To this man of intense faith God had made a promise that was now fulfilled.

Learning Activity 1

LOCATION OF THE TWELVE TRIBES IN CANAAN*
Refer to Joshua 13:8—22:34 to identify the location of each tribe in the promised land. Place the name of each tribe in the correct location on the map.

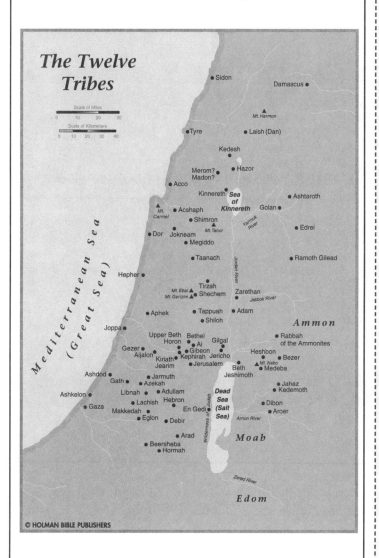

*For answers, see inside of back cover.

Caleb not only believed God but he also believed he could do something for God. Caleb had moved from what he could get from God to what he could give to God. We all need to be moving from what we can get to what we can give. Lives of significance come when we give ourselves in service to God. Caleb lived a life of significance through service.

<small>For Your Consideration</small> (14:1-15)

1. Which tribe did not receive a territorial inheritance? Why?

2. What land was given to Caleb?

3. Why had this land not been taken prior to Caleb's receiving it as an inheritance?

4. What characteristics made Caleb such an outstanding man of God for so many years?

5. How is Caleb a good role model for people who live at the beginning of a new millennium?

6. Do you have problems believing God will fulfill His promises to you? What areas of your life do you still need to turn over to God in faith?

7. In what ways does your faithfulness to God encourage other people to be faithful to Him?

Verses 1-5 summarize the division of the land. Two processes were followed in dividing the land. One involved the use of lots and the other involved God's promise given through Moses. Lots were used to determine how the inheritance on the west side of the Jordan River was distributed among the nine and one-half tribes while God's promise determined the land on the east side of the Jordan would go to the remaining two and one-half tribes.

The tribe of Levi served all of Israel as priests of the Lord. Since this tribe served all Israel, they did not receive an inheritance of land. They would not make their living from the land; they would receive from all the people. The Levites received cities to live in and land surrounding those cities for their livestock and property (vv. 3-4).

Since the Levites were not to receive an inheritance of land, why didn't just eleven tribes receive land? Israel did not have a Joseph tribe. Instead the descendants of his two sons—Ephraim and Manasseh—each received an inheritance of land. Thus the land was divided into 12 parts.

Caleb was of the tribe of Judah. Judah received some of the southernmost land available including land near the modern cities of Jerusalem and Hebron. In his request to Joshua, Caleb referred to the events of 45 years before when Moses had sent out the spies from Kadesh-barnea to determine how to take the land. Because of Caleb's faithfulness to God, Moses had promised to give Caleb and his descendants the land on which they had walked (v. 9). Caleb reminded Joshua of that promise. He wanted to receive the land and fulfill the challenge the Lord had given him.

Caleb lived by different standards than most people. He dared to be different. He looked at the opportunities rather than the problems. Caleb never changed. As a young man

Learning Activity 2

GOD'S PROMISES TO ME

Listed below are Scripture references to some promises of God. Place a checkmark by those already fulfilled in your life. Write a note describing when and how each was fulfilled. Use the last three lines at the bottom of the page to include other promises that are special to you.

PROMISE	FULFILLED?	WHEN AND HOW?
Psalm 32:8	_____	_____
Isaiah 7:14	_____	_____
Matthew 28:20	_____	_____
Hebrews 13:5	_____	_____
Revelation 3:20	_____	_____
Philippians 4:19	_____	_____
Romans 8:29	_____	_____
John 14:1-3	_____	_____
1 Thessalonians 4:16	_____	_____
Revelation 21:1-5	_____	_____
_____	_____	_____
_____	_____	_____
_____	_____	_____

he saw the promises of God and looked forward to fulfilling them. As he grew older, Caleb still wanted to fulfill God's purpose for his life.

IN DEPTH

Caleb, like Joshua, was among the 12 spies commissioned by Moses to spy out the land of Canaan and see how Israel could take it. All the spies agreed the land was fruitful and desirable. They also agreed the cities were well fortified and that among the people in Hebron and the surrounding hill country lived giants, the Anakim. Ten spies saw themselves as grasshoppers compared to the Anakim and believed there was no hope of taking the land. Joshua and Caleb presented another view. They said the giants were no reason for the people to be afraid because the Lord would give them the land. Israel accepted the report of the unbelieving spies, however, and refused to follow the Lord into Canaan. As a result the people wandered in the wilderness for 40 years until that unbelieving generation died. Also Caleb was promised he would receive the land around Hebron. Numbers 13—14 describes this incident.

Caleb had a forward look about him. I recently read about a study conducted of people who had lived to 100 years of age. Researchers wanted to find the common elements of such people. They expected to find these elements were diet or exercise or even heredity. They found only one common characteristic of people who had lived to age 100. They all looked forward. They saw the future as a challenge. Caleb had a spirit of perpetual youth regardless of his age (85). He believed he could take the land of the Anakim just as God had promised. Most important of all, Caleb believed God and believed God would fulfill His promises.

Caleb also accepted the challenge of difficult tasks. Caleb asked for the most difficult challenge of all. At first look Caleb's request appears to have been to receive an inheritance. He really requested to be given the most difficult job. The Anakim had intimidated the people of Israel. To this point their land had not been taken by the people of Israel. Caleb requested the challenge of taking the most difficult land possible.

Have you ever watched the early stages of work on a new skyscraper? Those who walk and work on the steel beams surely have one of the most difficult and dangerous jobs imaginable. Yet many people accept and do that job well. They could be called the Calebs of the construction industry.

Who is the "Caleb" in your church?

Who are the Calebs of today's churches? They believe the promises of God and they take on the most difficult tasks. Every pastor certainly knows and appreciates people like Caleb. Every church needs a Caleb. A church that has someone who will take on the toughest jobs is ready to make significant accomplishments for God. If your church has such a person, everyone in the congregation probably knows his or her identity.

One man wrote, "One must have a good memory to be able to keep the promises one makes."[2] I suppose that's one reason people don't always keep their promises. They don't remember all the promises they have made but that's no problem with God. He never forgets any of His promises. He also never fails to keep any promise He has made.

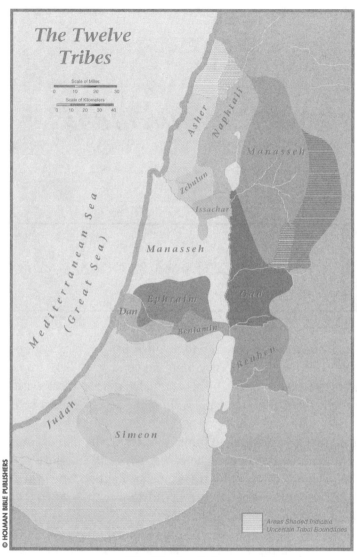

The Twelve Tribes

[1]Herschel H. Hobbs, *My Favorite Illustrations*, Ronald K. Brown, comp.
(Nashville: Broadman Press, 1990), 123.
[2]Friedrich Nietzsche, *Human, All Too Human* (Chicago: Charles H. Kerr
and Company, 1919), 95.

CHAPTER

7

Make a Commitment

Scripture Verses	Joshua 23:1—24:33 (Focal: 23:1-13; 24:1-24)

Several years ago a major world power took sides in a confrontation between two countries in the far east. Some mercenary soldiers from another country were enlisted to assist in this conflict. These soldiers were known for their "gung ho" attitude and usual willingness do anything asked of them.

The strategy called for these soldiers to jump from transport planes into combat areas to fight against the enemy. The officer who was in charge of them relayed this request, fully expecting the soldiers to agree. Since they had never been trained as paratroopers, they had the right to turn down the request. Unexpectedly, the mercenaries did just that.

The next day one of the mercenary's noncommissioned officers sought out the officer who had made the request. He reported they had changed their minds. They would agree to jump under certain conditions.

The mercenaries had three stipulations. They would jump but only into marshy or soft ground without rock outcroppings. They also wanted the plane to fly as slowly as possible. The commanding officer agreed with their first two requests, noting that planes always fly as slowly as possible when dropping troops. He did not accept their third condition, however. They wanted the plane to fly as low as possible, no more than 100 feet high. The officer explained this was impossible because the parachutes would not have time to open from that height.

Only then did the mercenary officer understand they would have parachutes. He then cancelled the conditions, saying they would jump anywhere with parachutes!

Would you jump with a parachute?

God has called us to the kind of commitment that says we will obey whatever He asks of us. Our commitment is to be such that we will go wherever our Lord wants us to go and do whatever He wants us to do.

What Has God Given Us? (Josh. 23:1-5)

A veterinarian and some assistants once tried driving a herd of cattle through a gate so the animals could be immobilized and medicated. The cattle refused to cooperate, however, and even became more stubborn the longer the men tried to drive them. Finally, while the men took a moment's rest, the cattle walked up to and through the gate. The men then successfully used this strategy to complete the task. They got the remainder of the herd to the gate but let them walk through it on their own.[1]

Joshua also used a similar strategy in addressing the people of Israel this last time. He didn't try to drive them to do what he wanted. He led them to do what God wanted by laying out the options before them and letting them make the choice.

Joshua certainly knew the people of Israel previously had made significant commitments to God. When they stood on the threshold of the promised land, they had made a commitment to follow God. They would not have taken the promised land without that commitment.

FOR YOUR CONSIDERATION (23:1-5)

1. What had God given the people of Israel?

Victory over enemies each tribe an inheritance in land

2. To whom did Joshua give credit for Israel's defeat of their enemies?

Lord had led them

3. What other promise from God did Joshua mention?

v. 5 *Lord, your God will expel them, drive them out + possess the land*

4. How do you think Joshua saw his role in Israel's success in the promised land?

5. What do you have that God has given you?

6. What do you have that God has not given you?

To introduce his new call for commitment, Joshua had the people to look back and remember how the Lord had led them in the past. Joshua reminded the people that God had given them the victory over their enemies and had given each tribe an inheritance in the land (vv. 3-4).

In a time of prosperity and peace, we can easily fall into the trap of believing we have created our own world and fought our own battles. How easily we forget that the Lord has led us and blessed us with His good gifts.

Though the victory was not yet complete, God promised to give the Israelites success over those tribes still remaining in the land. God promised He would fight for them in the future just as He had in the past (v. 5).

Now that the land had been sufficiently conquered and divided among the tribes, a new era was about to begin. The people needed to make new decisions about the future. New challenges and circumstances also call for new commitments from us.

David Livingstone, the great missionary to Africa, once received a letter saying some men wanted to come help him and asking if there was a good road to him. He replied, "If you have men who will come only if they know there is a good road, I don't want them. I want men who will come if there is no road."[2]

That was the kind of commitment Joshua called for from Israel and that's the kind of commitment God wants from us. You and I stand on the threshold of the third millennium A.D. If we are to make a difference in our world, we need to make this kind of commitment to God. The future may require courage from us but God will provide courage for those committed to Him.

What Does God Expect from Us? (Josh. 23:6-13)

As surely as the Israelites needed a reminder of what God had provided for them, they also needed to know what He expected of them. Joshua clearly stated those expectations. Joshua challenged the people to do all that is written in the book of the law of Moses and to love the Lord. He also specifically charged them not to associate with those other peoples who remained in the land of Canaan.

Joshua's command not to associate had nothing to do with prejudice, racism, or bigotry; it had everything to do with religion. Joshua knew the Israelites were not

Learning Activity 1

WHAT DOES GOD EXPECT?*

1. Joshua 23:6-8 has five instructions Joshua gave the people of Israel. In the left column below write the instructions. In the right column place a check beside those that are applicable to us today.

Instruction   Applies to me

a. _Be stRong_   _____

b. _Keep written in Book of lAw_   cAReful to obey

c. _No turn aside_   _____

d. _not associate with othe NATIONS_
   Not iNVoke NAmes of other's gods

e. _CliNg to the Lord_   _____
   Not seRve or bow to these gods

2. According to verses 9-13, what was the secret of the Israelite's success over great and powerful nations? How does this apply to us today?

_____

_____

_____

3. Why did Joshua command the people not to associate with the people of the land? How does this apply to us today?

_____

_____

_____

*For answers, see inside of back cover.

accustomed to the ways of the people of Canaan. These people based their religion on nature, a fact that accounts for its blatant appeal to immoral desires. The allure of such a religion posed a threat to Israel's allegiance to God.

For this reason God called for the people not to associate with these nations or to mention the name of other gods. Rather, the people were to cling to the Lord (vv. 7-8). The people had success because of their obedience. They had not taken the land of Canaan in their own right; their success had come through dependence on the Lord (vv. 9-10). Then Joshua called for the people to love the Lord and warned them of impending disaster if they refused to do what God expected (vv. 11-13). The people needed to remember that it does matter where you pitch your tent in life. If you pitch your tent in the wrong place, terrible consequences can follow.

Where you pitch your tent makes all the difference in the world!

SW PRODUCTIONS

When I was about eight years old, our family one time literally pitched our tent in the wrong place. We were traveling with the family of my best friend. We were so excited because we were going to go camping for several nights of the trip. My friend and I were to sleep in the tent with our dads. In contrast, because our four-year-old brothers were little, they had to sleep in the station wagon with our moms. We were so proud of our status—until disaster struck.

We camped one afternoon on a lovely green hillside. Since the weather was beautiful without any hint of rain, we didn't choose our spot for the tent very carefully. Nor did we dig a trench around the tent. After all, what could go wrong after such a beautiful day?

We soon learned everything could go wrong. During the night a severe thunderstorm struck the area. I had to hold up the corner of my sleeping bag to let the water run through the tent. I remember thinking how lucky my little brother was for getting to sleep in the station wagon! I learned that where you pitch your tent makes all the difference in the world!

As we get ready for the new millennium, we need to pitch our tents on the safe hill of commitment to God. Just as Joshua told the people of Israel, we need to obey the Lord, cling to the Lord, and love the Lord.

For Your Consideration (23:6-13)

1. What were the people of Israel to hold on to for the future?

2. Why was Israel not to associate with the people of the land?

3. According to Joshua, how does obedience to God relate to blessings from God?

4. Explain how Joshua 23:7 relates to God's command to make disciples of all nations.

5. Evaluate how well you are fulfilling God's expectations of His people.

Our choices determine our future. When we decide to serve the Lord, we put ourselves in the position to receive His blessings. When we decide to disregard His leadership, we put ourselves in the position to face the consequences of our decisions.

Whatever success I have in my own strength can make me feel smug and secure about my abilities. I have learned, however, that a life lived without God is not life at all. If I live apart from God, I experience only what I can produce on my own. If I live under God's guidance, I open up my life to all the good things God can provide.

How Has God Brought Us Here? (Josh. 24:1-13)

Someone has said you are never really a part of a family until you know the family's story. By that they mean you must know what has gone on in the past to understand how and why the family functions the way it does in the present.

SW PRODUCTIONS

"Tell me about the good old days."

When I was young, I never really cared to hear my dad or grandfather talk about the "old days." Now I find myself asking my father to talk about how he grew up and about my grandfather who died when I was young. There

Learning Activity 2

HOW HAS GOD BROUGHT US HERE?*

To discover what God had done in the life of the people of Israel, place answers to the following questions in the numbered blanks below.

24: 1-13

1. This group of ancestors included Terah, the father of Abraham and Nahor (24:2). Fathers of Israelites

2. This man was taken from the land beyond the River and led throughout Canaan (24:3). Abraham

3. The man in question 2 was given ___Issac___ (24:3).

4. This was the first son of the man in question 2 and also the father of Jacob and Esau (24:3-4).

5. God said after the people saw what happened to the Egyptians they _dwelt_ in the desert for a long time (24:7).

6. God told the people of Israel, "_land_ did not toil; _cities_ did not build; _A_ did not plant" (24:13). vineyards & olive groves

1. F U R e f A t h e R S

2. A b R A h A m

3. m A N y d e s c e N d A N t s

4. I S S A C

5. l i v e d

6. Y o u

The first letter of each word spells ___Family___.

*For answers, see inside of back cover.

is something incomplete in my life. I can better understand who I am by understanding who they were.

Joshua 24 begins by telling what God had done in the "old days." Joshua knew if the people could understand how God had worked in the past, they could see the importance of following God in the future. Joshua called the tribes of Israel to Shechem, which was roughly a central location for all the tribes (v. 1).

Joshua began his recitation of Israel's history with the call of Abraham from Ur of the Chaldees. The radical nature of God's call and the unwavering commitment of Abraham can be seen in the description of that experience. Abraham's father worshiped "other gods." Therefore, God called Abraham to leave his country and kin and even the gods his father had worshiped. God's call challenged Abraham to do a new thing (vv. 2-3).

FOR YOUR CONSIDERATION (24:1-13)

1. Where did Joshua call the tribes of Israel to assemble?

2. Where had Abraham's family originally lived?

3. Why did Joshua recite the history of Israel to the people?

4. To you, what is the most amazing event in Israel's history? Why?

5. What has God done to bring you to this point in your life?

6. What is the most amazing event so far in your journey with God?

Joshua then referred to Isaac and Jacob before proceeding to what God did in Egypt and at the Red Sea (vv. 4-7). Next he told how God brought the people to the east side of the Jordan River. There once again God gave the people victory (vv. 8-10). Joshua concluded the history by relating how God gave the people the land of Canaan and how God intervened directly to provide victory for the people (vv. 11-13).

MAIN BODIES OF WATER MENTIONED IN JOSHUA		
Body of Water	**Other Names Used**	**Scripture**
Jordan River	none	Joshua 1:2; many verses
Great River	Euphrates River	Joshua 1:4
Great Sea	Mediterranean Sea	Joshua 1:4; 9:1; 15:12,47
Red Sea	none	Joshua 2:10; 4:23; 24:6
Sea of Arabah	Salt Sea, Dead Sea	Joshua 3:16; 15:2,5; 18:19
Sea of Chinnereth	Sea of Galilee	Joshua 12:3; 13:27

What has God done to bring you to this point in your life? What has God done to bring your church to this place in its ministry? What has He done to bring us to the edge of 2000? More, what does He want us to do now and what kind of commitment will we make? *Refer to p. 83 cattle driven*

Whom Will We Serve? (Josh. 24:14-24)

Though history is important, the basic question of life involves more than what God has done in the past. The real question is: Whom will we serve?

The rest of Joshua 24 focuses on this question. Joshua reminded the people they could easily lapse into false ways of living. Instead of serving the God who holds the future, they could fall back into worshiping the gods from the past or they even could fall down before the gods of people around them.

Though it may sound strange, I believe a major challenge in the new millennium will be which god we will serve. Several years ago I read that in the future Americans would worship a combination of several gods. The article said this "god" would combine elements of Christianity, spiritism, eastern religions, a get-rich-quick mentality, and American patriotism with New Age emphases. When I saw that prediction over 10 years ago, I first reacted with "not in my lifetime." Now I see the validity of the prediction. On the eve of the 21st century, I see many of those elements in American religion.

Whom will you serve? Will you serve some popular god or will you serve the Lord your God in total commitment? Someone has said, "Most people wish to serve God—but in an advisory capacity only."[3] This was not the kind of commitment Joshua wanted of Israel. Neither is this what God wants of us today.

As we worship the Lord with all our hearts without turning to the right or to the left, we can move into the new millennium with courage for the future. To do that we need the "as for me and my house" mentality of Joshua. He expressed total commitment to God no matter what the future held for him.

FOR YOUR CONSIDERATION (24:14-24)

1. What response did Joshua want from Israel?

2. Who would be witnesses to the people's response?

3. Why is absolute allegiance to God alone important?

4. What evidence do you see that Christians today are in danger of forsaking the Lord for other gods?

5. How can you and your church help people understand the importance of giving God total allegiance?

6. What changes are you willing to make in areas of your life where you do not now demonstrate total commitment to God?

This kind of commitment has been expressed by other Christians too. When several of the poorest people in a village in India became Christians, 17 men in these families lost their menial, low-paying jobs. Their wealthy employers, adherents of another religion, refused to have Christians working for them, even though they paid them only what was then the equivalent of 10 cents per day.

For more than a month these Christians survived but barely. They even appealed to their former employers for help, saying their families were dying. Their landlords agreed to hire them back on one condition: they had to renounce Jesus Christ. Desperate, the men finally agreed. Because their wives and children were starving, they would participate in a ritual to indicate they were giving up the Savior.

The next day, as other Christians watched, these 17 men walked together to the pagan temple for the ceremony. Standing in front of the temple, they waited for the priest. When he appeared, he approached the first of the men and reached out to him. Surprisingly, the man didn't allow the priest to touch him, shaking his head instead. Each of the other men then did the same. The man who described this event added, "Jesus wouldn't let them go, and they turned back and went back to their village, back to their poverty, back to their hunger, back to their nakedness, back to their squalor and and dirt, back to Jesus Christ."[4]

That's the kind of commitment Joshua called for Israel to make. Have you made that kind of commitment?

[1]James E. Carter, *People Parables* (Grand Rapids: Baker Book House, 1973), 29.
[2]J. B. Fowler, Jr., *Living Illustrations* (Nashville, Broadman Press, 1985.) 29.
[3]Anonymous quote in Mark Link, *100 Stories for Special Occasion Homilies* (Allen, Texas: Tabor Publishing, 1992), 33.
[4]Clyde E. Fant, Jr. and William M. Pinson, Jr., *20 Centuries of Great Preaching* (Waco: Word Books, Publishers, 1971), 207.

CHRISTIAN GROWTH STUDY PLAN

Preparing Christians to Serve

In the **Christian Growth Study Plan (formerly Church Study Course),** this book *Joshua: Courage for the Future* is a resource for course credit in the **Reaching People Through Bible Study Projects and Groups Diploma Plan (LS-0053) and in the subject area Bible Studies (C6-0436)** in the Christian Growth category of diploma plans. To receive credit, read the book, complete the learning activities, show your work to your pastor, a staff member or church leader, then complete the information on the next page. The form may be duplicated. Send the
completed page to:

**Christian Growth Study Plan
127 Ninth Avenue, North
Nashville, TN 37234-0117
FAX: (615)251-5067**

For information about the Christian Growth Study Plan, refer to the current Christian Growth Study Plan Catalog. Your church office may have a copy. If not, request a free copy from the Christian Growth Study Plan office (615/251-2525).

Please check the course(s) you want to apply this credit. You may check both. ☐ C6-0436 ☐ LS-0053 (Sunday School)

PARTICIPANT INFORMATION

SOCIAL SECURITY NUMBER (USA Only)	PERSONAL CGSP NUMBER		DATE OF BIRTH (Mo., Day, Yr.)

NAME - FIRST, MIDDLE, LAST
☐ MR. ☐ MISS
☐ MRS.

| | HOME PHONE | |

ADDRESS (STREET, ROUTE, OR P.O. BOX)	CITY, STATE, or PROVINCE	ZIP/POSTAL CODE

CHURCH INFORMATION

CHURCH NAME

ADDRESS (STREET, ROUTE, OR P.O. BOX)	CITY, STATE, or PROVINCE	ZIP/POSTAL CODE

CHANGE REQUEST ONLY

FORMER NAME

FORMER ADDRESS (STREET, ROUTE, OR P.O. BOX)	CITY, STATE, or PROVINCE	ZIP/POSTAL CODE

FORMER CHURCH

| | CITY, STATE, or PROVINCE | ZIP/POSTAL CODE |

SIGNATURE OF PASTOR, TEACHER, OR OTHER CHURCH LEADER	DATE

*New participants are requested but not required to give SS# and date of birth. Existing participants, please give CGSP# when using SS# for the first time. Thereafter, only one ID# is required.